Delivering E-Learning

A complete strategy for design, application and assessment

Kenneth Fee

KOGAN
PAGE

London and Philadelphia

First published in Great Britain and the United States in 2009 by Kogan Page Limited

120 Pentonville Road
London N1 9JN
United Kingdom
www.koganpage.com

525 South 4th Street, #241
Philadelphia PA 19147
USA

© Kenneth Fee, 2009

ISBN 978 0 7494 5397 8

British Library Cataloguing-in-Publication Data

A CIP record for this book is available from the British Library.

Library of Congress Cataloging-in-Publication Data

Fee, Kenneth.
    Delivering e-learning : a complete strategy for design, application, and assessment / Kenneth Fee.
        p. cm.
    Includes index.
    ISBN 978-0-7494-5397-8
  1. Computer-assisted instruction. 2. Web-based instruction. 3. Educational technology.
I. Title.
    LB1028.5.F35 2009
    371.33′4—dc22

                                                        2008049559

Typeset by Saxon Graphics Ltd, Derby
Printed and bound in India by Replika Press Pvt Ltd

DISCARD

Contents

Introduction: Learning in the digital age   **1**
Katie, Devinder and Sam 1; Natives and immigrants 2;
Technophiles and technophobes 4; Learning through the
ages 5; Training and learning 6; About this book 6;
Introducing the Virtual Round Table 8; How to use this
book 9

1. Understanding e-learning   **11**
Common misconceptions 11; When research doesn't help 12;
A working definition 14; The three components of
e-learning 16; A different approach 17; The five models of e-
learning 20; E-learning 2.0 and learning 2.0 24; Summary of
key points 26

2. Advocacy of e-learning   **27**
Different thinking 27; Empowering learners 28; Expectations
and engagement 30; Benefits of e-learning 31; E-learning and
learning styles 33; Criteria for choosing an e-learning

List of figures

List of tables

About the author

Kenneth Fee began his career in the public sector and spent seven years as a training manager before the lure of the commercial world prompted him to switch to the supply side. In nine years, initially with the Open College, then, after its acquisition by Pearson plc, with Financial Times Management, he consulted with blue-chip clients, designed solutions based on published learning resources and provided management development using what we might now call a blended learning approach. He moved on to pursue interests in e-learning and knowledge management.

In 2001 his first book, *A Guide to Management Development Techniques*, was published by Kogan Page, and the same year he became Chief Executive of the eLearning Alliance. In 2005 he set up his own business, Executive and Professional Development Ltd, http://www.learnforever.co.uk, and now focuses on consulting, mainly around e-learning strategy.

Kenneth Fee has an MA, an MBA, and a professional Diploma in Training Management; he is a Chartered Fellow of CIPD and a Fellow of CMI. He is 48, married, and lives in Lanarkshire, Scotland, United Kingdom.

Foreword

If, like me, you have ever felt that you were drowning in an ocean of views, ideas, hype and myths about e-learning, then Kenneth Fee's book may be the lifebelt you need. From his early shot across the bows of the vendors who have 'effectively vandalized the market', this book gives the reader clarity in a field where clarity is a rare commodity.

Kenneth boldly claims that his book encompasses 'everything you wanted to know about e-learning but were afraid to ask!' With its mixture of checklists, web references and insight from sources around the globe, this book does live up to its promise. It demythologizes e-learning as 'the loneliness of the long-distance learner' and seeks to place it in the role of contributing to the empowerment of the learner. Boldly he states that 'e-learning is uniquely capable of helping generate a learning culture'. I suppose, as with me, when you hear this type of statement, alarm bells start to ring – yes, we have heard it all before! However, unlike some, he doesn't just deal in bold statements with little substance but goes on to explain how this can be achieved, with practical ideas and examples.

Tackling issues of learning style and preference head-on, he shows little sympathy for the 'technophobes' who seem to be able to package e-learning in a box labelled 'not for me', making a clear case that the 'digital natives' will shape the future of e-learning. For those of us who are resistant, the advice is, rather pointedly, become a 'digital immigrant' or retire!

However, Kenneth does not excuse the purveyors of bad e-learning and spends time looking at the learning design issues that need to be considered. He is passionate about good learning design and is clear that if we were attending a face-to-face training programme we would not be tolerant of a bad course – so why should things be any different for e-learning? His helpful tips, which will be familiar to the professionals in the field, but are all too often forgotten when 'going digital', are great reminders.

I am particularly attracted to Kenneth's view that e-learning should be seen within the wider context of learning rather than as an end in itself. Committing the time, resource and organizational effort to an effective learning strategy in which e-learning plays its part is vital. Too often the driver for most organizations has been cost saving disguised as 'going digital'. The outcome has been disillusioned staff lumbered with the latest product of a vendor – or, even worse, some poorly thought out e-reading!

The history of e-learning to date has been littered by great promise but disappointing delivery. With Kenneth's wealth of experience in learning and with the practical insights contained in this book, we may find that that disappointment becomes a thing of the past.

My only remaining question is… when does the e-learning version of the book become available? Or would that just be e-reading?

Bill McGrath
Scottish Enterprise

Acknowledgements

I should like to thank everyone whose work has been quoted or referenced in this book, and all those whose ideas have influenced my own, especially the 'Virtual Round Table' of international experts on e-learning: Marius Meyer, Nigel Paine, Serge Ravet, Allison Rossett, Martyn Sloman and Elena Tikhomirova. Thanks are also due to all those who provided advice and helpful comments, including Karen Fee, Jacqué Fee, Hannah Berry, and everyone at Kogan Page. Thanks to Mike Gillen, who was the first to seek my advice on e-learning; Kevin Grainger, who gave me my first e-learning opportunity; Paul Justice, who has helped me better understand some technology issues; David Elder, my supportive chairman at the eLearning Alliance; all my colleagues and clients; and, of course, Katie, Devinder and Sam.

My apologies to anyone I have inadvertently omitted to thank.

Introduction:
Learning in the digital age

KATIE, DEVINDER AND SAM

Katie is a 14-year-old schoolgirl who lives in the United Kingdom with her parents and her two brothers. Her father works in a factory and her mother in a shop, and she attends the local comprehensive school. She owns a mobile phone, a laptop computer, an iPod and two games consoles, and she uses them every day. She likes games and music; she exchanges text messages and instant messages with her friends; she takes photographs and has hundreds of them stored on her phone; she has her own page on the Bebo (Blog Early, Blog Often) website; she researches school projects on the world wide web, she is at ease with many computer applications, including Microsoft Word and Microsoft PowerPoint, and she types her school reports on her laptop and prints them off.

Devinder is just four years old and attends a pre-school nursery in the United Kingdom. She has a fascination with the gadgets her parents use, and likes to talk on the phone, although she has not yet learned (or been permitted) to answer it. However, she can confidently use the remote controls for the digital television and DVD player in her home, and the mouse for the family computer. Before she started nursery, she sat down with her parents and watched a DVD, which explained what it would be like and showed children playing there. At nursery she uses a computer, under supervision, as she is encouraged to look at things on the web. Although she cannot yet read or count, she can select images, sounds, and some letters and numbers, and manipulate them on-screen. Back at home, she has shown her grandmother the correct way to use a mouse, including practical demonstrations of how to 'click and drag'!

Sam is a 21-year-old student studying for a university degree in anthropology. She happens to be at a university in Britain, but it could be almost anywhere in the world. As with Katie, her personal arsenal of digital equipment includes a mobile phone, iPod and laptop computer. She also uses a games console, mainly for a karaoke application, but she also uses it to play movies on DVD. And she has her own page on the Facebook website.

Sam's university uses a learning platform called Moodle, through which she sends and receives e-mails from university staff, using her university-assigned e-mail address, accesses lecture slides and course notes, and takes part in discussions with other students. She connects to Moodle every day. Sam uses her laptop to type up assignments (typescript is mandatory for her course), and when in university she uses a desktop computer in one of the libraries, linking to Moodle, her funding and previous qualifications history, tutors' websites, online library catalogues, and other resources. Her entire academic career (and more) is underpinned by digital technology.

NATIVES AND IMMIGRANTS

Katie, Devinder and Sam are all digital natives. They are not exceptional: their stories have been selected because they are typical of young people almost anywhere. They have lived all their lives surrounded by digital technology and take it for granted. They find it as easy to use as a previous generation found telephones and wristwatches. It's a truism that if a technology has been around since you were born, then it's not 'new'; it's just something you accept, and quickly work out how to use like an expert.

As the examples of Katie, Devinder and Sam illustrate, today's young people have been using digital technology from a very early age: desktop and laptop computers, games consoles, mobile/cellular phones and other handheld devices, and all the connectivity of the internet. They use their phones to make calls, send and receive text messages, access websites, take and store photographs, and play games. They use the web for online game-playing, for 'social networking' (or, as one young person translated for me, 'to make friends and stuff'), to explore things that interest them and to create web space of their own. Most schools in the more developed countries, and even some in less developed countries, provide computers and internet access in the classroom, and e-learning is integrated into the curriculum of every university in the world.

This means young people have an expectation that digital technology will have an underpinning role in their work and learning for work. And woe betide the employer who does not fulfil this expectation!

I am a digital immigrant. When I graduated with my first degree, there were no personal computers and there was no internet. I first saw a computer in a workplace – complete with 5¼-inch twin floppy disk drives, one of which held the operating system – in 1983. I got my first desktop computer at work in 1992 and my first at home in 1994. By the end of that decade I was a regular user of e-mail and the world wide web, but these capabilities were more acquired than innate.

The terms 'digital native' and 'digital immigrant' arise from the metaphor of digital technology as a land you are either born to or move to. Many of us over the age of, say, 20 or so are immigrants (although some stubbornly remain aliens who never migrate to the new technology at all). The point is that our life experiences are very different from the life experiences of those who have lived all their lives with computers and the internet, and that means we respond to the technology in different ways. Table 0.1 offers some contrasting behaviours that highlight the differences.

However, some digital immigrants rapidly become immersed in the new culture, adopt digital native behaviours, and are just as responsive to the new technology as the younger generation. Such people become champions for applications such as e-learning, but they sometimes forget that not everyone shares their passion.

There have been many attempts to categorize the era we live in – the Post-industrial Age, or the Information Age, for example – but it can be hard to view our place in history without the advantage of hindsight. When I speak of 'the Digital Age', I'm not trying to classify an epoch,

Table 0.1 Digital native/immigrant comparison

Digital immigrant	*Digital native*
looks for a phone number in a directory	looks for a phone number on the web
prints off e-mails	subscribes to online magazines
writes a letter	sends an e-mail
makes a note of URLs	saves URLs to his or her favourites

merely to comment on the ubiquity of digital technology today, as distinct from just two or three decades ago. Perhaps in the not-too-distant future those steeped in the technology (natives or immigrants) will have a more apt name for this era.

TECHNOPHILES AND TECHNOPHOBES

As Carl Sagan said, 'we live in a society exquisitely dependent on science and technology, in which hardly anyone knows anything about science and technology'. This is not necessarily a bad thing.

I'm not a 'techie' – indeed, I have no special aptitude for science or technology, and little or no understanding of how microprocessors and telecommunications actually work. Which is fine – hardly anyone who switches on an electric light pauses to consider how the electricity is stored and transmitted, or would even know how to wire a switch. I work as an e-learning consultant, and I find people are sometimes surprised that I am not an expert in technology – but then they are usually reassured that my expertise is in learning, and you don't need to be a techie to understand how to apply technology to learning.

So, this book is not written for techies, or even for technophiles. Rather, it is for everyone involved in learning and development, regardless of how comfortable you feel about new technology. In fact, it is perhaps especially for those who are not particularly comfortable with it. Many works on e-learning seem written to help along those already embarked on the e-learning journey; this is useful, and I would like to think this book does it too, but I hope to offer something that will be accessible, and will have considerable appeal, to the novice or tyro, and will explain e-learning in language anyone can understand, and without assuming an extant frame of reference beyond a broad grasp of learning and business.

I remember seeing a cartoon in which a medieval warlord is preparing to do battle with his foes, with swords and shields and all the accompanying armour. Outside his tent he is depicted dismissing a salesman who is offering him a machine gun, saying that he doesn't have time to look at new inventions; he has a battle to win. This sort of image must be very comforting to technophiles who see themselves, like the machine-gun salesman, as unrecognized geniuses, ahead of their time, with the answers to everyone's problems if only they would stop and listen.

But that's not how everyone else sees it. Another cartoon shows a man perilously hanging by his fingernails off the edge of a cliff, while above him a boffin offers the reassurance that technology will save him. To the dangler, and to any reasonable observer, it is hard to see how. We need to acknowledge that not everyone sees the relevance, and that some people – technophobes, if you like – are intimidated by the array of strange new hardware and software, and all its associated jargon. This seems to me no less the case in e-learning.

Which of these cartoon caricatures is right will depend, from time to time, on the particular technology and the specific circumstances, but the lessons to take from them are that the technophiles are wrong to assume they have all the answers, and we have to try to consider the impact of new technology from the user's perspective.

LEARNING THROUGH THE AGES

This brings us to the question of learning. People have been learning since the dawn of humankind, initially mainly by discovery and experiment, trial and error, while organized learning, such as in classrooms, has taken place since antiquity. Much of our contemporary language of learning, including terms such as 'study', 'academia', 'university' and 'pedagogy', comes from classical Greece and Rome. In learning about learning, we are always discovering new concepts and re-examining our former precepts, but certain truths have held good for centuries, surviving the advent of new approaches to learning and the invention of new technologies.

Learning is first and foremost about *the learner*, and his or her will to learn. This simple truth is often lost amid concerns about the principles and practice of teaching or training, but in the latter part of the 20th century there was a resurgence of interest in 'learner-centred learning'. In the 21st century, e-learning has emerged, as shall see, as a means whereby learners can reclaim their position at the centre of learning.

Learning is also about *purpose*. Aims and objectives. Applications to real life. As T H Huxley said, 'The great end of life is not knowledge but action.' Learning may be a virtuous circle, or an end in itself, but its meaning is always about what we do after we learn, about learning how to do things better than we did before. This is particularly true of learning for work, which strives for behavioural change, functional competence and organizational improvement. Effective learning for work has clarity of purpose as its compass.

There have been many historical milestones in learning, such as the innovation of Plato's Academy in Athens; the foundation, in medieval times, of the first great universities of Europe; the development of printing that popularized the written word and gave generations access to books; literacy campaigns throughout the ages; and, in the 20th century, educational broadcasting via radio and television. In the past quarter of a century the invention of the microprocessor, combined with the development of internet communication, threatens to represent the most significant milestone yet.

As the examples of Katie, Devinder and Sam show, e-learning is already having a huge impact on the formal education of our young people, from the kindergarten to the university. It is also revolutionizing informal learning, as people find it much easier to source information on the world wide web, to communicate by e-mail and to conduct research projects, large and small, as they wish. Our focus in this book is on learning in the world of work.

TRAINING AND LEARNING

For a long time, learning for work was described stiffly as vocational education or, more commonly, as training. I am fond of quoting the late Anita Roddick's saying that 'training is something they do to dogs'. It was never a term that inspired, or offered a sense of ownership. Training increasingly sounds too directive, too didactic, diminishing of the learner, and like a dreary obligation. So, this book will not talk much about vocational education or training, but rather about learning – and about e-learning.

There are still some who consider learning for work a narrow and dull field compared to the more wide-ranging fields of learning for academia or research, and for personal development and enlightenment. This may be partly because in the past, training was delivered in dull ways. But the scope of learning for work is enormous and encompasses some of the most fascinating subjects in the world, while making a clear and significant contribution to wealth creation and the furthering of human knowledge, understanding and capability. In a small way, this book is part of that noble undertaking.

A big part of what I have to say is that in the digital age, companies that do not embrace digital technology in all aspects of their business, including learning, will fail. This stark truth needs to be more widely recognized, accepted and acted upon. This book aims to equip businesspeople to do that.

ABOUT THIS BOOK

This book describes a new and better way of understanding e-learning, overcoming objections to e-learning, and acknowledging poor past practice while pointing to a better new approach. It places the emphasis firmly on learning, not the technology; it demystifies the jargon and debunks industry myths. It is deeply critical of vendors who have misled and overcharged customers and effectively vandalized the market.

This book describes in detail how to devise and implement an e-learning strategy, including how to align it with a general learning strategy and overall business strategy. No other book on e-learning to date has focused on strategy, and hardly any have been written from a strategic perspective.

This book provides a unique insight into how to manage e-learning effectively and serves as a reference manual for those interested in looking up specific aspects of e-learning. It is written for a professional and managerial audience and is especially relevant to the reader in a corporate environment. It offers a fresh perspective on a subject that is still widely misunderstood and misapplied, despite being in vogue in many organizations.

There are seven main chapters in the book. Chapter 1, 'Understanding e-learning', provides an introduction to the language, considers why e-learning is widely misunderstood, discusses how to understand it better and shows how to make the most of it. This chapter offers definitions, identifies the components of e-learning and describes different models of e-learning.

Chapter 2, 'Advocacy of e-learning', asks why so many attempted e-learning implementations have failed. It looks at how to recognize and overcome objections, and how to influence effective e-learning implementations. This chapter offers a distinctive tool for advocating e-learning, the Impact Matrix.

Chapter 3, 'E-learning strategy: development', explains how to develop an e-learning strategy from scratch, how to align it with overall learning and business strategies, and how to ensure that it is meaningful and effective. This is the foundation of implementing successful e-learning.

Chapter 4, 'E-learning strategy: suppliers and resources', sets out to demystify digital technology for learning. It examines how to classify suppliers, then work out how to make the most of them and integrate them into your strategy.

Chapter 5, 'E-learning strategy: learning design issues', offers a new way of looking at how to design e-learning. It explains how it is different from learning design for other media, points out the pitfalls of poor e-learning design and shows what to do to make it work well.

Chapter 6, 'E-learning strategy: measurement and results', considers the variety of different approaches to learning evaluation, how they apply to e-learning, and whether they actually work. It shows how evaluation must be inextricably linked to strategy development.

Chapter 7, 'Learning more about e-learning', points out where to go for further information, where to find support, and how to undertake self-development in e-learning. This chapter includes web references and an annotated bibliography.

The book concludes with an epilogue that offers some thoughts, speculation, forecasts and predictions, followed by a glossary of technical terms used in relation to e-learning.

INTRODUCING THE VIRTUAL ROUND TABLE

While researching this book, I interviewed a number of leading representatives of the e-learning community from around the world. My idea was to talk to a range of people from different countries and different professional backgrounds, a group who ought to have different perspectives and insights on e-learning issues. I was not disappointed. Their thoughts and comments are spread throughout the book, and clearly attributed. The points where they diverge are intriguing, while the points where they converge help demonstrate that the ideas and opinions I express in this book are not necessarily unique to me, but in many cases are shared by many others. (This is not a disclaimer. Ultimately, I accept full responsibility for everything in this book that is not specifically attributed to someone else.)

The following list identifies these representatives.

Marius Meyer is a South African academic, HRD section head of the University of South Africa, board member of the American Society for Training and Development (ASTD) Global Network South Africa, and a founding member of the Institute for Organisation Development and Transformation (IODT).

Nigel Paine is an expatriate Briton who temporarily lives in Australia but works all over the world. He is former head of People Development for the British Broadcasting Corporation, a visiting professor at Napier University, and on the advisory board of Wharton Business School Learning Leaders Doctoral Programme. He runs his own company, which focuses on people, learning and technology.

Serge Ravet, a Frenchman, is chief executive of the European Institute for E-Learning (EIfEL), former vice-president of the European Foundation for Quality in E-Learning (EFQUEL), and president of EventFolio.

Dr Allison Rossett is an American, Professor Emerita of Educational Technology at San Diego State University, California, and a former member of the boards of directors for the American Society for Training and Development and the International Society for Performance Improvement (ISPI).

Martyn Sloman is a Welshman, a visiting professor at Glasgow Caledonian University in Scotland and Kingston University in England, and Adviser, Learning, Training and Development for the United Kingdom's Chartered Institute of Personnel and Development (CIPD).

Elena Tikhomirova, a Russian, is chief executive of E-learning Center, based in Moscow. E-learning Center is a leading Russian company developing customized content and providing consulting services on e-learning implementation.

I interviewed these international experts separately, but asked them all the same questions. Their responses appear throughout the book as 'Virtual Round Table' discussions.

HOW TO USE THIS BOOK

This book is designed, to borrow a piece of e-learning jargon, as a linear experience: it is intended to be read from start to finish, and the chapters follow a natural progression. However, it is possible to dip into some sections more selectively: Chapters 3–6 (inclusive) are about how to create and implement an e-learning strategy, and each of them may be consulted independently, although you will find a number of cross-references. But in any case, as with any work of reference, feel free to consult it as you see fit. It should encompass 'everything you always wanted to know about e-learning but were afraid to ask'! More specifically, this book aims to help you implement successful e-learning and I hope it achieves that aim.

There is a summary of key points at the end of each chapter, and, as already noted, a bibliography in Chapter 7, which also offers some suggestions for further investigation and study. This book also features a series of glimpses into the experience of a learning and development manager setting out to apply the ideas of this book and implement e-learning for the first time. These provide a practical example of our theory. I hope this book stimulates you to think more about, and look further into, e-learning, and make it a significant part of your personal development. We need more clear thinking on e-learning, and we need more champions.

I live and work in Britain, and inevitably many of the experiences I draw upon, and examples I use, are from the United Kingdom. Equally inevitably, no matter how hard I try to maintain a global outlook, my idiom surely remains distinctively British. But I hope and believe the lessons of this book are universal and can be readily understood and applied anywhere in the world. I welcome feedback: please contact me by e-mail at ken@learnforever.co.uk, via my blog at http://learnforeverblog.blogspot.com, or via my LinkedIn network at http://www.linkedin.com.

Illustrative project: Introduction

Katharine Roberts is a learning and development manager with a leading UK retailer. This is her story of how she implemented successful e-learning:

It all started when the HR Director called me into his office and told me we were doing an employee survey and using focus groups to get a better understanding of staff attitudes. He suggested we should include some learning-related issues.

I had a think about it and decided to recommend some open questions about how people like to learn, what sort of things they like to do, and what they don't like. Some of the results were predictable, but we noticed a significant trend of referencing social networking websites, and when we explored this further with the focus groups, we found very high usage of digital technology by almost all of our younger employees – and some of the older ones too.

Our business is committed to exploiting digital technology to improve performance and add value, so it makes sense to look at how we use it to help our people learn more effectively. As we got into it, we began to realize we needed to provide more e-learning opportunities.

1

Understanding e-learning

This chapter begins by trying to correct some of the mistaken and incorrect thinking about e-learning that is all too prevalent, and bemoans the lack of good general reference material on the subject. From there, it builds a picture of what e-learning is really about, explaining that it is an approach, not a method, and creating a new working definition. It explains the three component parts of e-learning, describes five different models of e-learning and discusses some different learning blends. Lastly, it debunks some of the worthless jargon that does not help our understanding of e-learning. Along the way, we hear for the first time from the members of our Virtual Round Table, on what they think are the big issues in e-learning.

COMMON MISCONCEPTIONS

Too many people think e-learning is about the loneliness of the long-distance learner. When they think about e-learning, they often conjure up an image of a solitary individual sitting at a keyboard, working his or her way through readings, exercises and tests. They think of it as distance learning, and they think of it as self-study, lacking the interactions and the 'human dimension' of more traditional ways of learning.

This view of e-learning then leads to a lot of misconceptions. From this flawed frame of reference and stereotyped image, people derive a view of e-learning that is as inaccurate as it is limited.

Anyone moved to design e-learning in this way should reflect that information and communication technology (ICT) ought to be used to support and improve learning experiences, not replace them with a poor substitute. Some people have experienced e-learning that conforms to this stereotype, and this has engendered hostility to the very concept of e-learning. But it is a mistaken hostility, based on the wrong kind of experience.

I have met many people who say, 'I don't like e-learning' or, in a slightly more sophisticated version, 'it doesn't suit my learning style'. I'm always amazed by these statements. Nobody would go on a bad course and come away saying, 'courses don't work for me' – or, if they did, nobody would take them seriously. Another analogy would be people who said they wanted to learn but they didn't like reading books. No employer would accept that as a reasonable explanation for not consulting an instruction manual. And yet this sort of attitude to e-learning persists – although perhaps not for much longer, as the digital natives take over and the alienated either become digital immigrants or retire.

A notable misconception is that only certain knowledge, or limited skills, can be gained by e-learning. While it is true that some e-learning methods are better suited to knowledge acquisition rather than skill development, the inferred conclusion about the limits of e-learning, in all its forms, simply does not follow. In this chapter and the next, we will explore why. For the moment, let's say that there is much more to e-learning than many people imagine.

Some readers may feel they already understand e-learning, and will be inclined to skip this chapter. I hope not. To quote Doris Lessing, 'That is what learning is. You suddenly understand something you've understood all your life, but in a new way.' I aim to help people understand e-learning in a new way.

In this chapter we look at what is really involved in e-learning, what it means, and how it works. We consider the interrelationship of the components of e-learning, and we look at different e-learning models in order to reach a more complete understanding.

WHEN RESEARCH DOESN'T HELP

Clarifying the meaning of the word 'e-learning' itself is a good place to start. In my research, none of the standard works of reference has been much help. Most British dictionaries of English do not include a discrete entry for e-learning, simply offering e- as a prefix denoting electronic. The exception is the Collins dictionary, which describes e-learning as a computer-based teaching system. Learning and development professionals, who understand the distinction between learning and teaching or training, need better information. The good people at Collins are forgetting the great dictum of Galileo Galilei: 'You cannot teach a man anything. You can only help him discover it within himself.'

But perhaps this should not be surprising, as the modern concept of e-learning, and even the term itself, is not much more than a decade old. According to the etymology in Webster's American English dictionary, the term first appeared in the year 1997. Some attribute to veteran e-learning commentator Jay Cross the credit for having coined it, but nobody seems able to cite the exact reference to prove this claim. It happened at a time when people were adding 'e' as a prefix to many common words, including e-mail, e-business and e-commerce. What is certainly true is that the term was very rapidly adopted, and became common currency all over world by the turn of the century.

However, there has never been much agreement on how to spell 'e-learning', let alone how to define it. The main spelling variations are e-learning, eLearning (the choice of the European Union), elearning and e-Learning. Further variations italicize the e. And the leading British journal on the subject idiosyncratically spells it e.learning (to be fair, this is a branding foible that does not extend to the spelling in the body of the journal).

Some people argue that we should not distinguish e-learning from learning in general, as doing so encourages the view that it is a separate phenomenon (a view that some e-learning vendors have encouraged). They reason that e-learning should be subject to the same disciplines and the same measurements as any other form of learning. A related, but separate, argument is that the term should not be used at all, as e-learning is just another form of learning, albeit in electronic form. The standard retort to this is that the term 'e-mail' has been used for much longer and is still usefully distinguished from traditional mail that is physically delivered ('snail-mail', as the techies derisively call it). These objections to even discussing e-learning recur all the time, diverting and stifling debate whenever they arise.

Whether e-learning is a term that will be used in the future is not a question that will be encountered in this book. I start from the acceptance that the term is in current use, and seek to explain what we understand by it. I hope to demonstrate in this chapter and the following one that e-learning is a distinct subcategory of learning, and one that can help us reach a better understanding of learning overall.

E-learning is widely misunderstood. To the layperson, its specialized vocabulary is often mystifying. But not just that: people who debate its pros and cons sometimes find themselves arguing at cross purposes, because they are referring to different things. There are different kinds of e-learning, which we shall shortly distinguish, but learners who have experienced only one kind are not in a position to make judgements about the overall benefits.

One indicator of the confusion around the subject can be found in the fragmented entry on e-learning in Wikipedia, the free encyclopedia that anyone can edit. Between the time of my writing this and when you read it, that entry will have been edited and re-edited a number of times, but my guess is that it will still be an enigma, wrapped in a puzzle, inside a conundrum. Rarely has a new concept, the subject of so much attention, been so muddled.

For further evidence, consider the unhelpful glossary of terms provided by Wikipedia (at least, as I write this in 2008) – an arbitrary selection not even listed in alphabetical order.

A WORKING DEFINITION

There are too many definitions of e-learning. Many are offered by vendors, and should be treated with some suspicion, as they will be written to place the vendor's offer at centre stage. Academic definitions, and those provided by governmental and professional bodies, are more authoritative, but still quite diverse, and sometimes more relevant to a formal educational setting than to a corporate context.

According to the European Union (EU):

> eLearning is the European programme in the field of ICT for education and training which promotes the inclusion of ICT in all learning systems and environments (formal, non-formal, informal – school, higher and adult education and training).

In other words, the European Union defines e-learning in terms of practical EU initiatives, and takes a very broad view. But one weakness of this description is that it tells us very little about what ICT actually offers learning.

The American Society for Training and Development (ASTD) is the world's biggest professional body for learning and development, with about 70,000 members in about 100 countries all around the world. This makes it arguably better placed than most to define what e-learning is. The ASTD originally defined e-learning like this:

> e-learning covers a wide set of applications and processes, such as Web-based learning, computer-based learning, virtual classrooms, and

digital collaboration. It includes the delivery of content via Internet, intranet/extranet (LAN/WAN), audio- and videotape, satellite broadcast, interactive TV, and CD-ROM.

This is a rather technology-specific description, likely to date, and liable to confuse all but those who already know what it is.

That was from 1998. By 2001 the ASTD was ready to expand somewhat on that:

E-learning refers to anything delivered, enabled, or mediated by electronic technology for the explicit purpose of learning. This definition excludes things that might fit under the title 'distance learning', but are non-electronic (such as books and paper-based correspondence). It is broader than, but includes, online learning, Web-based learning, and computer-based training. E-learning includes both one-way and two-way learning exchanges, as well as learner-to-learner interaction (as occurs in learning communities). For simplicity, assume that if you use a computer in some fashion to affect learning, then it is e-learning.

This is more useful, if a bit self-referential, but we need to encapsulate the concept in a briefer statement.

The United Kingdom's Chartered Institute of Personnel and Development (CIPD) manages greater brevity when it states that e-learning is:

learning that is delivered, enabled or mediated using electronic technology for the explicit purpose of training in organizations.

The CIPD uses this definition to clarify the meaning for respondents to its regular surveys, hence the closing emphasis on organizations. This remains useful for our consideration of learning at work, but adds an unnecessary addendum to a general definition that can be used by all; we do not need to have a different definition for the world of work from what would be useful for schools and universities, and for e-learning for personal development.

Our definition needs to demonstrate and clarify some of the thinking needed to correct misconceptions. It should say something about the phenomenon that is e-learning, without recourse to examples, and should embrace all the technological applications, while excluding extraneous detail. It should also be as jargon-free as possible, expressed in simple, plain English. Therefore, we arrive at the following working definition:

E-learning is an approach to learning and development: a collection of learning methods using digital technologies, which enable, distribute and enhance learning.

That much should be clear enough. Some people want to engage in futile argument over whether true e-learning is purely online, or whether any learning that uses computers is 'e'. Instead, we should agree that there are different kinds of e-learning, and seek how to classify them and thence to understand them better.

THE THREE COMPONENTS OF E-LEARNING

Allison Rossett distinguishes the 'stuff' of e-learning from the 'stir' – the stuff being the content, and perhaps the bits of technology that go into the mix, and the stir being the way the learning is put together, the connectivity, the teaching or training approach, the overall design. This is a useful distinction, because it makes people think about what goes into e-learning and how it all fits together. But we can go further.

There are three component parts of e-learning, namely enabling technology, learning content and learning design (see Figure 1.1). People tend to focus on the first, the technology, because this is the new and unfamiliar component, but the other two are at least as important. Software vendors tend to place great emphasis on the first, because that is what they contribute, and where they make their living, but that does not mean that learning and development professionals need to follow suit. Chapter 4 will look at the technology in more detail.

It almost goes without saying that the content of any learning programme is important, but it is a mistake to elevate it to prime importance. The phrase sometimes used is 'content is king', but it shouldn't be. Technologists frequently underestimate what is involved in learning, seeing the learning process as little more than manipulation of content. And sometimes vendors emphasize the primacy of content to flatter the buyer and to protect their technology. Their concept of learning is as a process for transferring knowledge from A to B, like the traditional sender–receiver model for communication (see Chapter 5 for further explanation). Thus, they reason that effective e-learning is just about combining technology and content. This is a good formula for providing information online, but there is a lot more to learning.

The 'more' is in the third component, learning design. Some people refer to this as pedagogy, but this is bad jargon, derived from inappropriate Greek (the first syllable of the word refers to children, whereas we are concerned with adult learners, and the correction 'andragogy' would be

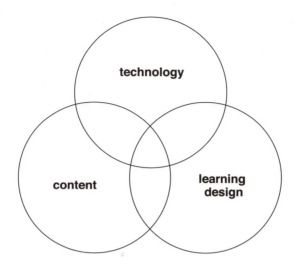

Figure 1.1 The three components of e-learning

further mystification, as is the latest fad for 'heutagogy', or self-directed learning). It is not enough simply to automate information in order to achieve learning; we need to understand how people learn, and how best to manage the learning process to achieve improved performance at work. As Elliott Masie says, 'If we don't focus on the experience dimension of learning, we run the risk of mistaking the publishing of information for learning and training.'

Good e-learning is therefore a combination of technology that works, meaningful content and effective learning design. These three components complement one another and need to be carefully combined: the design needs to make the most of the content, and the technology needs to enable both the content and the design, if it is to work.

For learning and development professionals, accessing content and technology from other sources, the design component then becomes the most important. We shall explore this in more detail in Chapter 5.

A DIFFERENT APPROACH

Perhaps the most important point to grasp is that e-learning is more than just another method or technique like, for example, distance learning or action-based learning. Rather, it is an approach – an aggregation of various methods made possible by the latest digital technologies and those yet to come. It is about harnessing those technologies, incorporating them into existing learning methods and drawing upon them to reconsider the use and effectiveness of those methods.

Self-study online is a learning method. E-assessment is a learning method. A synchronous online learning event is a learning method. Consulting an online instruction manual is a learning method. Undertaking an online simulation is a learning method. There are many more learning methods within the e-learning family, and there will be more in the future. Collectively, these methods represent a different approach.

If you examine the classic training and development cycle, with its four phases of needs analysis, planning, implementation and review, where does e-learning fit? (See Figure 1.2.)

Mainly, it seems, in the phases of planning and implementation. E-learning has so far had little to offer to the phases of needs analysis or evaluation and review, except in so far as common, standardized electronic tools may be offered to assist these processes – and to date the only ones of note are generic survey tools. It is an indication of how little software developers understand learning and development that these phases have been, hitherto, largely ignored. It follows that these may well be areas for future development of e-learning.

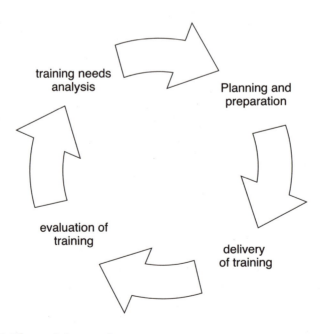

training needs analysis

Planning and preparation

evaluation of training

delivery of training

Figure 1.2 The training cycle

E-learning is therefore an approach to traditional learning and development activities that embraces new thinking associated with new technologies, with an emphasis on planning and implementing learning interventions, and managing them – and appreciation of the potential of these technologies informs our understanding of learning in general.

Virtual Round Table: Part 1

I asked each of our international experts what they thought were the big issues in e-learning at the moment.

Allison Rossett said, 'The big issue in e-learning is what is it? What is the definition? Is it tutorials or scenarios online or is it much, much more? Is it knowledge management? Is it performance support? Is it e-coaching? I say yes and advocate a big-tent view of e-learning.' Serge Ravet expressed a similar view when he said, 'It is the definition of e-learning itself. The UK government was smart when it moved from strategies for e-learning to e-strategies for learning. E-learning is not a domain like open and distance learning, it's a delivery mechanism. We should be looking at how technology is transforming learning.'

This is in accord with a key theme of this chapter: that we need to get to a shared, better understanding of e-learning. The other issues identified were different, but they all help us to reach that understanding.

According to Nigel Paine, 'There are three big issues: getting the environment right – and that includes getting the right LMS [learner management system] or CMS [content management system] in place; trying to integrate more informal processes like blogs and wikis into more conventional delivery platforms; and finally the big one: user-generated content – how to encourage it, how to quality-assure it and how to incorporate it.'

Marius Meyer thinks, 'The big issues revolve around the technology–human interface: getting the right technology according to the needs of the target market. Getting people involved in e-learning remains a big challenge.

'E-learning is not about technology, it is about people. Change management is therefore of utmost importance. Communication and involvement of all relevant stakeholders is absolutely critical throughout the process.

'Despite the fact that the use of e-learning in South Africa (30 per cent of companies) compares quite well with the situation in the USA, there is still a very high "don't know" rating that seems to indicate that many companies are not sure how to go about e-learning in South Africa.'

Elena Tikhomirova focused in on the practicalities of implementing e-learning. 'I believe that the biggest issue in e-learning is motivation. When deploying e-learning in both corporate and academic sectors, the first thing we have to keep in mind is the reason why people will sit in front of the computer spending their time instead of going to a face-to-face event with a teacher present, in person. Another big issue is media selection. With so many different technologies available, people try to enrich courses with many different kinds of components. Unfortunately, not all components are effective and they often disturb learners rather than help them to achieve the objectives of the learning. And the last, but not the least, issue I want to mention is goals. In a classroom, uncertain goals can be covered with additional information from the teacher; but in self-paced e-learning, learners need a road map that will help them to reach desired learning outcomes. This can be only achieved by having clear goals and objectives for the course, written in the language suitable for the target audience. Learners need to see what is in this course for them, and how it can help them to make their work or private life better.'

Martyn Sloman sums up: 'E-learning has arrived and has become a key part of training provision. We are entering a new period of transition. We are moving from a focus on the stuff to a focus on the stir.'

THE FIVE MODELS OF E-LEARNING

Pioneering work in this field was brought to light by Martyn Sloman, who described the following typology in his seminal 2003 book *Training in the Age of the Learner*:

- web-based training;
- supported online training;
- informal e-learning.

The first of these, *web-based training*, is the classic online learning formula, which some would hold to be the only true e-learning. Sloman describes it thus: 'Content is delivered to the learner without significant interaction or support from trainers, managers or other learners.' Of course, this type of delivery can be made not just via the web, although that is the most common mode, but via intranets or corporate networks, or simply stored on a PC hard drive or a disk. Sloman observes that, historically, this model is derived from computer-based training (CBT), widely available since the 1980s.

The second model, *supported online training*, also has a historical derivation, from open or distance learning, and is what many people describe as 'blended learning' – what used to be called mixed-mode or mixed-media learning. As Sloman observes, 'blended learning' is a bit of a misnomer, and usually refers to blended *training*. It may be argued, since all learners blend the inputs and influences that are useful to them, that the expression is no more than a tautology; all learning is blended. But regardless of nomenclature, it is a recognizable model, in which 'the learner interacts intensively with the tutor and other learners, supported by online content as appropriate'.

At this point we must digress. There are a number of different forms of 'blended learning' worthy of being distinguished. Here are just four:

- *The sandwich*. The course sandwich is one classic blend, where pre- and post-course work is offered online. This is online learning with a 'traditional' course as the sandwich filling.

- *The milestone*. Another classic form is to start with an online course and add on face-to-face training events (group work or one-to-one) as milestones, which help to pace the programme.

- *Knowledge and skill*. A third form is to use the online part of the blend for underpinning knowledge while using a face-to-face approach for skill development.

- *Complementary resources*. The fourth form sees online learning resources offered as back-up to face-to-face training, allowing learners to refer back to coursework when they are on the job. In this form, the online part is subservient to the offline, but it is a blend that often works well.

There must be many other forms, and many others may emerge as we become craftier at blending training and learning resources.

To return to our categorizing of models, you should avoid picking a favourite model of e-learning; they all have their place. Also, you should note that e-learning does not have to be blended to be interactive. The first model can provide interactivity with tutors, managers and other learners, with 'virtual tutors', and with interactive features of the technology itself.

The third model, *informal e-learning*, Sloman describes as deriving from knowledge management, but this would be a parallel rather than a historical development. 'The learner employs technology to communicate with colleagues and learn during the normal course of work.' Sloman's tag 'informal learning' seems rather vague and excludes the more formal expressions of this model, such as when organizations offer learning banks or other online resources for continuous professional development (CPD). The defining characteristic seems to be that the learning is self-managed or, if you prefer, it is the application of knowledge management for learning.

However, Sloman's typology ignores at least two more extant models. A fourth is *live e-learning*, in which we have live synchronous learning events – sometimes called 'webinars' (a contraction of 'web-based seminars') – with learners in a variety of locations participating together at a prearranged time. This sounds rather like 'web-based learning', Sloman's first model, but it is the antithesis of what he defines as that model (as it clearly does not lack 'significant interaction or support'). It also sounds a bit like 'supported online learning', but it lacks the offline dimension of the second model.

The discovery of this fourth model prompts us to revisit the names we give to each one. 'Web-based training' is an insufficiently precise label for the first model, which really comprises online coursework to the exclusion of anything else. Similarly, 'supported online training' does not accurately define the second model, nor distinguish it from the fourth; the second is really about blended learning, although that label too is imprecise. And 'informal e-learning' does not do justice to the organized process of utilizing online resources for self-managed learning. Let's finish the list, then apply some new labels.

A fifth model is *electronic performance support* (EPS). This is the term for instruction available in the workplace, perhaps incorporated into a computerized system designed to perform a task, or perhaps held by the operative as an electronic form of instruction manual (for example, on a handheld device). We should be wary of including any or all forms of technology-assisted information provision as learning models, but this one seems to allow genuine scope for learning and development, through interrogation options, as opposed to simple operational instructions about 'which buttons to press'. Conceivably, EPS could include live contact with a tutor or mentor to discuss, for example, an unusual situation.

And so we have five models: online courses, integrated online and offline learning, self-managed e-learning, live e-learning and electronic performance support. These are summarized in Table 1.1.

Having established this, we must admit that this is not necessarily a definitive classification of e-learning models. There may be more than five. The situation is fluid, and in the light of experience new models may well emerge – indeed, some may already be with us.

For example, it is possible to argue that the digitally resourced classroom represents another model of e-learning. The EU and ASTD definitions certainly would lead to this conclusion. Instead of traditional chalk-and-talk, the modern classroom or training room equips trainer and learners with a battery of digital aids – not just presentation software, but networked terminals, projectors and touch-sensitive screens, allowing for sharing of audio and video clips and other files. This is like model 4, live e-learning – only actually face to face.

With this potential sixth model, it becomes apparent that the pervasive nature of digital technology is such that no method or approach to learning can be free of it. Just as the classroom benefits from the support of digital technology, so too does work-based learning, with access to equipment in the workplace; and so too does coaching or mentoring when the participants use digital communication devices.

The distinction we need to make is that some models are only possible thanks to the technology, while others can work with or without the technology. By this measure, the digital classroom is merely a variation of classroom-based learning, not a new model. But live e-learning is a

Table 1.1 The five models of e-learning

Model 1	online courses	exclusively online courses, providing learning solely via the internet
Model 2	integrated online and offline learning	learning programmes that integrate online learning with complementary offline activities
Model 3	self-managed e-learning	the provision of online learning resources for self-managed learning
Model 4	live e-learning	synchronous online learning events involving learners in multiple locations
Model 5	electronic performance support (EPS)	work-based online learning to support specific tasks, systems or operational procedures

radical departure from the face-to-face situation of a conference or seminar. It is true that there are historical versions, technology-free, of some of the models, but the new models have rendered these archaic. The older versions that survive, such as print-based open or distance learning, remain discrete learning models beyond the scope of e-learning.

We should remain alert to the possibility of further models emerging as e-learning continues to evolve. And whichever model(s) we use, we should be aware of the potential of each in itself, and not constantly try to relate it to other learning models. A common mistake of people new to e-learning is to think of it as automated distance learning, or an electronic book, or whatever. Like thinking in one language and translating into another, this is a limiting mindset. We should focus on the new medium and the new model.

Looking forward, we should consider the application of different e-learning models to different situations and needs in our organizations. Some will be suitable in some circumstances, and the role of the learning and development professional is to make this sort of decision.

To complete our understanding of e-learning, we have to acknowledge more recent – and unhelpful – jargon that has become all too commonplace.

E-LEARNING 2.0 AND LEARNING 2.0

The term 'e-learning 2.0' has emerged to refer to the use of social software or 'shareware' such as blogs and wikis. However, the term is unhelpful. It arises from a desire to characterize the latest e-learning as being so differentiated from old e-learning as to represent a new and much better generation. This is a highly questionable claim – especially since it refers just to the use of supporting technology rather than to the learning content and the learning design. However, the main problem is that it deliberately uses software jargon to mystify the subject for those not familiar with such 'technobabble'. Anyone who uses the term 'e-learning 2.0' should be challenged to clarify exactly what they mean.

I believe the concept of e-learning 2.0, like many new terms that have sprung up in e-learning, is motivated by vendors' desires to distance their products from perceived and real past failures of e-learning. In fact, the limitations and the misapplication of these products, or earlier versions of them, are among the reasons why previous implementations of e-learning failed.

The specific new technologies associated with e-learning 2.0, such as discussion forums and blogs, are actually not new at all. These tools were very much a part of 'e-learning 1.0' (which, incidentally, is a rarely heard term, since it would demand a definition, which would expose the emperor's new clothes of e-learning 2.0). What has changed is that more people have become comfortable with using the technology and have learned how to make the most of it. From this has sprung the greater degree of learner input and participation, and the consequent improvement of learning models. It is disingenuous in the extreme for software vendors offering essentially the same products to claim any credit for a movement that has grown in spite of them.

Learning 2.0 is an even worse piece of jargon. It implies that people now learn in different ways – which, of course, they don't. People have new opportunities, arising from new learning methods, and this may improve our perception of how people learn, and help us understand it better. But human brains have not evolved in any significant way. People still learn in the same ways they always did.

The genuine substance underpinning the emergence of these two pieces of jargon is the phenomenon of social networking. But even this is not really new. What is (relatively) new is awareness of its potential, and media hype surrounding it. People are increasingly using the web for social networking, but links being claimed to applications for work seem spurious. Neither the terms nor the underpinning concepts of e-learning 2.0 and learning 2.0 help us understand e-learning any better.

I shall conclude this chapter, and the others that follow, with a summary of the key points that should help us reach a better understanding of e-learning.

Illustrative project

Taking the decision to go down the e-learning route was the easy bit. But exactly what sort of e-learning would work for us?

I knew what one or two of our competitors were doing, and I wasn't impressed. One of them had converted printed workbooks to an online format, and what I'd seen of it looked dull and uninspiring. I'd also seen PowerPoint slides on web pages, and even with audio commentary and the odd video clip thrown in, I knew that wasn't for us.

What had worked quite well for us in the past were CD-based learning resources with lots of video content, so we wanted to build on that, but offer much more interactivity and more learner support. We decided on a blended learning model with a variety of resources online and support both from a central group of tutors *and from mentors in each of our stores. We felt that, with the right tools and the right support, the learners would start to create their own learning network, just as we'd seen they did on social networking sites.*

I now had a pretty clear idea of what sort of e-learning to implement, but I knew it would take time and resources, and to proceed I needed to secure high-level commitment and a new budget.

SUMMARY OF KEY POINTS

1. There are many misconceptions about e-learning, most notably a narrow view of what it is, derived from the limited scope of early e-learning implementations.

2. Our working definition of e-learning is that it is an approach to learning and development, a collection of learning methods using digital technologies that enable, distribute and enhance learning.

3. E-learning has three distinct but complementary components: enabling technology, learning content and learning design.

4. E-learning is best understood as an approach to learning, not a method. It is an aggregation of a number of related methods. It is an approach that is undervalued, and promises greater potential for all aspects of learning for work.

5. We can identify five discrete models of e-learning: online courses, integrated online and offline learning ('blended learning'), self-managed e-learning, live e-learning and electronic performance support (EPS).

6. There are many different ways of blending online and offline learning, which we can recognize as the milestone, the sandwich, the knowledge and skill blend, and the blending of complementary resources – and probably many others.

7. Some superfluous jargon has emerged under the banners of e-learning 2.0 and learning 2.0 to try to express the potential of social networking for learning. But this jargon does not help most people understand e-learning any better.

2

Advocacy of e-learning

This chapter moves on from looking at e-learning as a different approach and considers it an entirely different way of thinking about learning. It describes the way of thinking that should be shared in any organization. It offers learning and development professionals a set of information that can support this new thinking, and some techniques for bringing it about, and introduces a specific tool for winning support for e-learning. Our Virtual Round Table reconvenes, and offers opinions on what works well, and not so well, in e-learning.

DIFFERENT THINKING

In Chapter 1 we saw that e-learning is more than just a method of learning; it is a broad approach, encompassing many methods. Now I want to take that further and say that e-learning is not just a different approach to learning but a new and different way for organizations, and people within them, to think about learning.

There are a number of old ways of thinking, one of the most popular being to identify problems that require training solutions, and then pass them on to the training department so that the training specialists in that department can arrange a course. A better way (but not much better) is to pass the problem on so that the training 'experts' can identify the appropriate training intervention: if not a course, then some coaching, or guided work-based learning, or an action learning set, or perhaps some distance learning or online learning. Of course, another way, sadly still common, is simply to ignore learning issues until they become too urgent to ignore any longer.

More forward-thinking organizations have recognized that these ways are not adequate. They place responsibility for learning and development not upon training specialists whose role is to inform and advise, and to enable and facilitate learning, but instead on all managers and, ultimately, on the learners themselves. Such organizations are striving to attain a learning culture or build a learning organization. E-learning is an approach that makes this easier to achieve, by encouraging learners to take control of their own learning, by making learning more learner centred and by empowering learners.

The philosophy of learner-centred learning makes the learner the focus, sees everything from the perspective of the learner, and fosters the development of learning resources and interventions that put the learner first. This means analysing and determining learning needs in terms of the individual learner's needs; it means writing learner objectives from the learner's point of view; it means getting learners active in the learning process and allowing them to choose how they learn; and it means involving learners in planning and reviewing learning. It means much more, too: it is the learner-centred philosophy that makes possible both a learning culture and a learning organization.

EMPOWERING LEARNERS

A learning culture is a climate within an organization where people enjoy learning and see it as one of the benefits of working there – where people welcome and seek out opportunities to learn, and work is often arranged to build in learning experiences. By definition, a culture is not really a tangible thing, but we can identify distinguishing characteristics to help us know when we have one. Peter Senge is the organizational development theorist who has had most to say about this. He has identified five dimensions of a learning culture: personal mastery, mental models, shared vision, team learning and system thinking (see Table 2.1).

A learning organization is one that already embodies the five dimensions in Table 2.1, and where systematic learning is aligned with work to ensure lessons are learned as jobs are completed, and the organization is better equipped to face the challenges of the future. Senge defines a learning organization as one 'where people continually expand their capacity to create the results they truly desire, where new and expansive patterns of thinking are nurtured, where collective aspiration is set free, and where people are continually learning to see the whole together'. This implies individuals having a great degree of

Table 2.1 A learning culture

Dimension	Description
personal mastery	creating an environment that encourages the development of personal and organizational goals in partnership with others
mental models	using visualization or 'internal pictures' to help shape behaviour and decisions
shared vision	winning group commitment by developing shared images of how the future should look
team learning	encouraging collective thinking and working, so that a group's capacity to develop intelligence and ability is greater than the sum of its individual members' talents
system thinking	developing the ability to see the 'big picture' within an organization, and understanding how changes in one part affect the whole system

control over what they do, and being encouraged to experiment, explore and, above all, learn.

The philosophy of the learning culture and the learning organization underpins successful e-learning. When we look at how e-learning works, we see that the empowerment of learners takes a number of forms:

- They have greater choice over when they start e-learning.

- They can learn at their own pace, at times and in places that suit them.

- They can exercise greater choice over what they study, or at least what they prioritize.

- They can choose the training inputs that best match their learning styles.

- They themselves can contribute inputs to the learning process.

- They have access to the broadest range of resources, and some of the richest resources at that.

- And, contrary to conventional wisdom, they should have _more_ opportunities for interaction.

E-learning is capable – indeed, I would argue that it is uniquely capable – of making this empowerment possible. Certainly, good e-learning should embrace all of these points. I would go further and argue that e-learning is uniquely capable of helping generate a learning culture and build a learning organization. However, no amount of theorizing can prove that; you need to experience it happening in your own organization. This is the 'big picture' that e-learning advocates need to work towards.

An implicit but important step in promoting this empowerment is the dedication of substantial corporate networks and systems to employee development, which sends a potent message about how employees are valued. This is not just about the financial investment; it shows that the organization is thinking and behaving differently, and is in tune with the lifestyles and aspirations of its employees.

EXPECTATIONS AND ENGAGEMENT

In Gardner and Holmes' 2006 book *E-learning: Concepts and practice*, the authors succinctly express the new reality: 'e-learning requires different types of engagement'. In other words, learners behave differently – are required to behave differently – when using e-learning. This represents a challenge (and accounts for some of the resistance to e-learning), but it also means we reap new benefits. And Gardner and Holmes mean not just that the engagement in e-learning is different from what has gone before, but that e-learning is multifaceted and demands a variety of different ways of engaging.

New employees in our organizations arrive with new expectations. As we have already observed, young people especially use computer and internet technologies in every aspect of their lives. They have their own desktop or laptop PCs, probably of a higher specification than they are being offered at work, and have been accustomed to using them since early childhood. Their home connection speeds to the internet may actually be faster than those at work. They have their own, increasingly sophisticated, mobile phones and handheld personal entertainment devices such as iPods, and use them constantly. They are experienced electronic game-players, using many different consoles. They participate in online communities via websites such as MySpace, Bebo, Facebook, Flickr and YouTube, and countless message boards and chat rooms. They frequently have their own website in addition to their space on social networking sites. Employees like this are not going to be satisfied with the old ways of learning (or working); they expect a lot more.

The digital natives are not the only ones with new expectations. The digital immigrants, who are discovering how the technology can revolutionize their lives, are just as demanding. There have been – and still are – those who resist digital technology, but they are becoming a smaller and smaller minority. For the new majority, e-learning is not just desirable but essential.

And the new expectations are not restricted to employees. Other stakeholders share the same life experiences and will share the same perspectives. At home, employees' families are immersed in digital technology. Customers will expect their suppliers to utilize e-learning, and vice versa. Shareholders and prospective investors will consider the company's investment in digital technology for learning and other purposes, and similar pressures will come to bear on public bodies from committees, politicians and lobbyists.

If this is all starting to sound revolutionary, we need to be careful to retain a sense of proportion. I am not saying that e-learning is the only approach to learning. There will continue to be situations that benefit from other approaches, notably a technology-less work-based approach, or the one-to-one support of coaching, mentoring and counselling, or the traditional classroom-based approach, or some of the new innovative approaches that are being deployed. We need to be able to identify the circumstances where e-learning is the best approach, but we also need to recognize that e-learning is the way of thinking most closely associated with a learning culture and the learning organization.

The beginnings of successful advocacy of e-learning within an organization occur when everyone begins to accept this new way of thinking. It is not enough for learning and development professionals alone to have this enlightened understanding. Everyone, including not just employees but all the stakeholders I have identified, has to begin to see learning and e-learning in a new light. Everyone has to get engaged in the e-learning project.

BENEFITS OF E-LEARNING

It is important to reach a shared understanding of the benefits of e-learning. We can readily identify various circumstances when e-learning ought to be especially useful, such as when:

- There is a need to implement a more or less standard learning programme on a large scale.
- There is a need to deliver learning within a short timescale.

- Face-to-face methods would be cost-prohibitive.

- There is a frequent need to update or amend the learning content.

- Learning content requires a significant degree of personalization.

- There is a need to coordinate diverse elements such as on-the-job activities, simulations, readings and assessments.

- Learners are looking for self-managed solutions.

- Learners show a preference for working and learning with digital technology.

This is by no means an exhaustive list of when e-learning works well, but it is intended to demonstrate that there are a variety of appropriate situations and contexts.

Early vendors of e-learning emphasized cost savings as the key benefit, and it is true that e-learning, like distance learning before it, offers opportunities to avoid the costs of delegate travel, subsistence and accommodation, and the hire of training facilities – non-training costs that often dwarf the training fees themselves. However, these vendors soon found themselves trapped in a cul-de-sac, as such savings can be made only once (there may continue to be a cost advantage of e-learning over face-to-face learning, but once the savings have been cut from the budget, they're history). Another emphasis of early vendors was on economies of scale, and there is no doubt that e-learning lends itself to large-scale implementations, but this was more a way of vendors targeting a top slice of the market than an analysis of what e-learning does well. Moreover, this emphasis may have discouraged small businesses, which, it should be stressed, have just as much to gain from e-learning.

E-learning can:

- make learning possible – or affordable – in circumstances where other approaches are not feasible;

- save on costs;

- deliver learning faster;

- leverage greater value from corporate ICT investments;

- make better use of learning opportunities already available on the web;

- exploit learners' enthusiasm for digital technologies;

- be very adaptable to change, through speed of publishing and updating;

- offer a highly learner-centred solution.

And if you accept the argument from Chapter 1 that e-learning represents not merely another method but a whole new approach to learning, then a key benefit should be that it makes you think differently about learning and opens up a range of new possibilities.

I do not propose to labour the arguments about each specific benefit of e-learning. These have been elaborated on elsewhere (see the references in Chapter 7), and in any case will vary in their application: certain killer arguments in one context will seem spurious in another. A useful exercise is to test each claim in your own setting by comparing each claimed benefit for e-learning against the benefits offered by alternative approaches. This will strengthen your conviction regarding what the real benefits are for your organization, and what really makes a difference. And it should encourage a healthy scepticism towards some of the over-hyped claims of disingenuous vendors.

E-LEARNING AND LEARNING STYLES

In my 2001 book *A Guide to Management Development Techniques*, I argued that e-learning can offer something for every different learning style preference. This should be true for all forms of employee development, not just management development, so let me see if I can prove that.

There are many competing models of different learning styles and style preferences. Let's focus on what are (arguably) two of the best known and most widely adopted.

The starting point for what may be the longest-established model is David Kolb's experiential learning cycle (see Figure 2.1). Kolb's original idea, in 1984, was that learning can be divided into four phases – experiencing, reflecting, conceptualizing and experimenting – and that all learners go through these phases continuously and repeatedly, in a cycle. In the 1990s, Peter Honey and Alan Mumford moved on from this to develop the idea that each learner tends to have a preference for one of the four phases, hence a 'preferred learning style'.

The four types of learners, as proposed by Honey and Mumford after Kolb, were thus activists, reflectors, theorists and pragmatists:

- *Activists*. These learners prefer to concentrate on doing things, and accumulating concrete experience. This type of learner emphasizes the top left-hand part of Kolb's cycle, 'experiencing'.

- *Reflectors*. The learner who likes to spend time reviewing his or her experience and reflecting upon problems, perhaps measuring experience against theory, characterizes the top right-hand part of the cycle, 'reflecting'.

- *Theorists*. A learner who takes the most cerebral approach, the opposite of the activist, and focuses on understanding concepts is a theorist whose behaviour corresponds to the bottom right-hand part of the cycle, 'conceptualizing'.

- *Pragmatists*. The learner who likes to plan, explore options and test theories is a pragmatist whose behaviour corresponds to the bottom left-hand side of the cycle, 'experimenting'.

Nobody is suggesting that learners fit rigidly into just one category, but if these are distinct styles, perhaps even preferred styles, then the question that arises is whether e-learning can fulfil the expectations of learners who prefer each style. My answer is yes, and here are some examples:

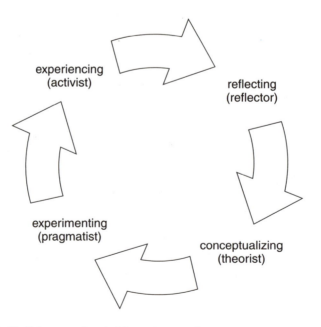

Figure 2.1 Kolb's experiential learning cycle

- Games, practical exercises, quizzes and any of the activities that may be built into e-learning meet the needs of the activist.

- Examples of e-learning approaches that would suit the style of the reflector include comparison of case studies with the learner's own experience, and work-based assignments, perhaps with online feedback.

- The theorist is perhaps the easiest of all to deal with in an e-learning setting, through the provision of readings, and perhaps other resources such as audio and video clips.

- Finally, the pragmatist benefits from simulations and fluid examples that may be manipulated by the learner to experiment with different possibilities.

The other leading learning styles model is simpler, being based on how we perceive things through our biological senses. It is derived from Colin Rose's work on accelerated learning, is closely related to the ideas of Neuro-Linguistic Programming (NLP) and traces its roots back to early-20th-century ideas about the education of children, such as the Montessori Method. Think of the old saying, attributed to Confucius, 'What I hear, I forget. What I see, I remember. What I do, I understand.' This model distinguishes three main learning styles: visual, auditory and kinaesthetic or tactile (see Table 2.2).

Again, we can find examples within e-learning to fulfil the expectations and preferences of each type.

The visual style is straightforward. E-learning gives us text and pictures, video and animation, a variety of rich and dynamic content to offer a feast for the eyes.

The auditory style can be accommodated through the use of sound in audio and audio-visual clips, and through oral/aural communication with tutors and other learners in a live e-learning situation, such as a virtual classroom (see Chapter 4).

Lastly, the tactile type is a bit less straightforward, and the chances are that this learning style preference will be better served by means other than e-learning, but there are practical activities online, including simulations, and the sense of touch may be stimulated by the use of various interfaces, not just a keyboard and mouse but perhaps a games joystick or a touch-sensitive screen.

In short, e-learning can stimulate most of the senses (the obvious exceptions, so far, being our senses of smell and taste – although I wouldn't rule out the possibility for the future), can address every conceivable learning style preference, and may actually offer the best possible option for certain styles, can work with individual learners and interactive

Table 2.2 Learning styles

Learning style	*Description*
visual	looking at things: watching and reading
auditory	not just listening, but speaking as well
kinaesthetic/tactile	doing things, and using the sense of touch

groups, and can satisfy an enormous range of learning circumstances. In comparison with other approaches and methods of learning, which can be quite restrictive and limited in their suitability for different styles, e-learning proves to be extremely flexible and effective.

CRITERIA FOR CHOOSING AN E-LEARNING APPROACH

When to opt for e-learning is a matter of judgement. There is no simple formula for decision making, no matrix on which to plot points in favour of one or another approach. However, the five steps that follow represent a useful checklist for deciding whether to adopt an e-learning approach. The five steps, in order, are learning needs, learner style preferences, cost, time and value-add, as represented in Figure 2.2. This sequence is not immutable. There may be situations, for example, where time is of the essence, or where a low-cost solution is paramount. But all else being equal, the steps should be considered in the sequence given.

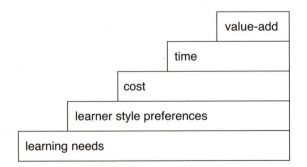

Figure 2.2 Criteria for choosing e-learning

1. Learning needs

What learning needs are under consideration? Is it possible for these to be addressed by e-learning? Are there ways in which the learning lends itself to a particular approach? It is likely that most learning needs can be addressed by more than one approach, or combination of approaches, but some may require a special approach. If so, the rest of this checklist can be ignored, as the issue of meeting learning needs should have primacy over everything else.

2. Learner style preferences

Do you know anything about how the particular group of learners like to learn? If so, can an e-learning solution take account of these preferences? Bear in mind that different e-learning models can offer something for every, or nearly every, learning style preference.

3. Cost

How does the cost of an e-learning solution compare with other approaches? Usually, rough estimates will enable you to determine which approach should be least costly. Later, combining this consideration with step 5 will enable you to determine which approach should be most cost-effective.

4. Time

Is there any time pressure on implementing the learning? If so, does e-learning help or hinder? Can you compare how quickly the learning can be launched and how long implementation of the learning solution will take, using different approaches?

5. Value-add

How is the learning going to be evaluated? (See Chapter 6.) How will you measure its impact? Does this influence the learning approach?

This checklist may be used when e-learning is being considered, as a means of confirming whether it is the right approach. Or it can be used in a more neutral way, to test a choice of approaches before deciding which one is the best fit.

Virtual Round Table: Part 2

I asked each of our international experts to consider what works well and what doesn't work so well in e-learning, and to highlight any particular examples that have impressed them recently. For a start, let's look at what they think works well.

Elena Tikhomirova highlighted interactivity: 'In my opinion the biggest benefit of e-learning is the possibility of learners' interactions with content. At the same time, people can learn and practise, solve problems and be active in the process of their learning.'

Allison Rossett highlighted value and relevance: 'Most important in my view is *great* value delivered when and where needed. So, it's not the form of the e-learning that's number one for me. It's the usefulness, the link to what the individual needs to be successful.' Martyn Sloman agreed that 'when content is relevant to the organization, and is well designed', it works well. Martyn also stressed that 'e-learning is more effective when combined with other forms' and that 'e-learning demands new attitudes on the part of the learner'.

Serge Ravet took a historic view and argued, 'What worked well in open and distance learning still works well in e-learning, only further enhanced by the technology. Computers can multitask. But that's just formal learning. Informal learning is more interesting – and has more potential.'

Serge's point about multi-tasking is an important distinction between e-learning and some of the older approaches and methods. A computer user can easily work on more than one thing at once, perhaps reading documents intermittently while answering e-mails, or taking part in an instant messaging conversation while viewing video clips. Clearly, there is a limit to how easily we can combine reading, writing, drawing, listening, watching and other activities, but the essential truth is that multimedia enable multi-tasking.

Marius Meyer and Nigel Paine turned their attention to practical issues. Marius noted the poor technology infrastructure in some parts of the world and argued, 'E-discussion groups work quite well, because they probably require technology that is not too sophisticated and is readily available in Africa. Proper guidelines and support systems are needed to make e-learning work.' Nigel emphasized 'mass delivery very quickly; you can get to everyone at once. The flexibility of doing it when you want to, not when someone tells you to; the ability to cut and paste good material to save for later; the ability to go back over material and reuse it or re-acquaint yourself with it; and the flexibility of being able to break out of the non-linear. Go where you want and prioritize what you choose to prioritize.'

The range of views underlines the point that e-learning has many benefits to fit many situations.

On the debit side, the round table members found plenty of examples of bad practice too. Serge went back to 'Old models; push, not pull; constraints of curricula, subject barriers and constant testing.' 'Technology,' he said, 'is about liberating learning.'

Marius disparaged technological fetishes in a couple of different ways, including 'technology that is too sophisticated and requires a lot of people to log in at the same time. Start-up costs are quite high, so some companies are hesitant to commit resources if they are not convinced about the return on investment. Dumping technology without the necessary guidance and support is also problematic. Many companies in South Africa have wasted a lot of money buying expensive systems from the USA and other countries, yet these systems were not seen to be relevant to the African context.'

Allison cited the perpetual problem of people attempting short-cuts such as 'taking PowerPoint presentations and putting them online in the hope that folks will read them, or read and listen'. And Elena agreed: 'E-learning is not suitable for transferring big amounts of text. It needs a lot of work to split all information into bits and pieces suitable for online delivery. Another thing that doesn't work well is chat that has limited capacities in terms of people that can be present there at the same time. But despite all the pitfalls of e-learning that I've mentioned, I believe that all instruments and technologies that are used now and then in e-learning work well when incorporated in the course to help learners to achieve the goals of learning. Each instrument must have its own application in the course and should be used only when it will be most effective and not because that instrument is popular or is available.'

Martyn summarized nicely: e-learning doesn't work well 'when content is not so relevant, and is not well designed'.

As for specific examples that have impressed our experts, some spoke of certain methods that they had seen work well, while one or two cited very particular examples. The latter included Allison's vote for UC Davis Virtual Hallucination Clinic in Second Life, and Martyn's for Hilton University.

Elena said, 'My biggest impression in e-learning recently was my discovery of the Articulate rapid e-learning tool. When I started using it I would never have thought that course creation could be such an easy and pleasant process. The tool has a highly user-friendly interface and it is very intuitive, so anyone with any level of knowledge can start creating a course after 10 minutes of studying the instrument.'

For Nigel, 'some of the latest work we did at the BBC was superb in terms of user engagement and involvement and creating as far as possible real-world solutions'. He has also been impressed by 'some of the materials that use gaming techniques or simulation to build up pressure and authenticity in real time'.

Serge opted for 'e-portfolio developments (but not portfolios for their own sake)'. He believes that 'outside the world of formal education – creating knowledge, sharing and blogs – schools and universities look increasingly like museums or antique shops'.

Lastly, Marius commented that 'different companies in South Africa use different systems, and most of them seem to work. E-discussion groups work quite well in South Africa and other African countries, provided that people have access to computers'.

INFLUENCING PEOPLE

When seeking to introduce e-learning to their organizations, learning and development professionals are trying to initiate a significant change. Leading change always involves winning hearts and minds, and never more so than when everyone is going to be personally involved, not just in how they are expected to behave but in how they are expected to think and learn.

The successful advocates of e-learning will have to see their role as leading change, and enact a change management plan. This should involve identifying all the forces for change, and all the barriers or forces of resistance, then formulating a plan for the forces of change to overcome the forces of resistance. It should involve identifying allies and finding ways for them to influence others; and it should involve identifying key individuals who may hold hostile views that need to be challenged and changed. It will not be a single great act, but an accumulation of lots of events, activities and discussions over a period of time. Implementing this change management plan will not be quick or easy, but in most organizations, winning support from senior management, and making the plan explicit, should help accelerate the process.

You will need to acquire and use influencing skills. These include the ability to express ideas clearly and to offer a vision; to avoid being confrontational (except as an occasional tactic); to recognize and respect others' points of view, and seek to accommodate them where possible; to consider what motivates others, and find ways to show a match with your goals; to convey enthusiasm, which can be infectious; and more. This is not an exhaustive list. You need to avoid making it personal, and make the issue the needs of the organization.

Perhaps the most important lesson for advocacy of e-learning is that argument can carry you only so far; what you really need is solid evidence, and the best way to generate that is by implementing successful e-learning and letting it speak for itself. Let the real-life example of e-learning be your influencer. As Albert Einstein said, 'Setting an example is not the main means of influencing another, it is the only means.' A well-designed piece of e-learning, based on sound technology and content, and responding to a clearly identified need, will be that example, because it will provide a successful business solution.

What many vendors have done wrong is to sell their products rather than try to find solutions to their clients' problems. (They often make a point of claiming the opposite, but judge them by their actions, not their words.) These vendors have taken short-term and selfish views into the market, which is understandable and can often be the driver of competition and progress. But in many cases it has meant vendors have misled buyers – who, in turn, have allowed themselves to be misled – into accepting an understanding of e-learning specific to one particular model, if not (worse still) specific to a particular vendor's product.

Of course, this is akin to the advice for travel directions that says, 'To reach your destination you shouldn't start from here.' When you begin to make the case for e-learning, you lack the benefits of a good concrete example, and until you can create one, your focus must be on winning the more abstract argument.

THE PARADIGM SHIFT

In many organizations, what we need to achieve to get people thinking differently, and more positively, about e-learning is a *paradigm shift*. A paradigm is a shared mindset, in our case about what e-learning is and what it can achieve, and a value judgement about whether it is any good. The shift is about dramatically changing these shared basic assumptions, in our case to a new, broader and more optimistic view of what e-learning is and what it can achieve.

We need a paradigm shift from the caricature of e-learning as a narrow set of isolated learning activities, unsuitable for many learners and many learning situations, to a new vision of e-learning as a broad approach to learning in the digital age, encompassing rich and dynamic possibilities, engaging learners and looking to the future. We will not achieve this shift simply by insisting that we are right and everybody else is wrong, but rather by involving people in discovering the potential of e-learning for themselves. Let us therefore construct a model that demonstrates the potential of e-learning and that people can apply to their own experiences. We shall call this model the Impact Matrix.

THE IMPACT MATRIX

The popular perception is that e-learning is best suited to factual, knowledge-based learning rather than anything involving skill development or attainment of competence. According to this narrow view of e-learning, it has limited capacity to influence behaviour change or performance improvement, or to help learners and organizations strive for excellence. But that is not a fair perception.

If we construct a simple two-by-two matrix, we can plot learning on one axis as more or less knowledge focused or skills focused. All skill development includes some underpinning knowledge, and all knowledge includes at least some cerebral if not manipulative skill. Thus, knowledge and skill are not polar opposites, but two extremes of a single dimension. If we see knowledge-to-skills as a continuum, we can determine whether a piece of learning is more factual or informational, or, towards the other end of the continuum, is more about developing skill. This is the horizontal axis, and is shown in Figure 2.3.

On the other axis, we can consider whether what needs to be learned tends to be a common, widely shared need, or whether it tends to be specific to the needs of a particular organization, yielding a generic-to-bespoke continuum. Again, in real life hardly anything is entirely generic

knowledge   skills

Figure 2.3 Knowledge–skills continuum

or completely bespoke. Most things exist somewhere along a continuum between the two extremes. This continuum is represented by the vertical axis shown in Figure 2.4.

When we bring these two axes together, we form a classic two-by-two matrix with four broadly distinguished categories represented in each of the four boxes. This is the Impact Matrix, and is represented by Figure 2.5. The symbols in each box, explained in the paragraphs that follow, are derived from the Boston Consulting Group's famous growth-share matrix used for business strategy consulting since the 1970s (or at least, three of the four symbols are; the other one owes more to Monty Python or *The Da Vinci Code*).

The lower left-hand box of Figure 2.5 is for more generic, more knowledge-based learning. This is where the overwhelming majority of the e-learning market has been to date (and thus has skewed perceptions of e-learning), because it is the easiest form of e-learning to package and sell. If we refer back to the five models of e-learning in Chapter 1, this is typically model 1, or occasionally model 2. Generic courseware vendors, notably large publishers, developed this market from the late 1990s onwards, often migrating catalogues of CD ROM-based, or latterly DVD-based, courses to online versions. As this is where vendors continue to make most of their money, this is represented in the diagram as a cash cow.

Figure 2.4 Generic–bespoke continuum

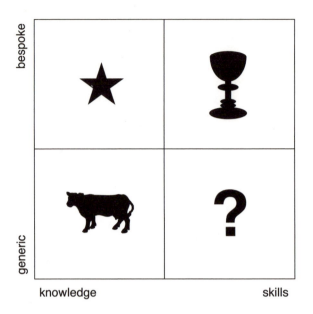

Figure 2.5 The Impact Matrix

Few vendors have developed courseware that would fit in the lower right-hand box of the diagram, as this is more difficult, and more expensive, to do. It would also involve engaging more closely with learning and development professionals to better understand the learning needs of their client organizations, and this is a strategic path vendors have, regrettably, eschewed. Generic courseware has concentrated on knowledge-based, not skill-based, learning, leaving a legacy of doubt that there is a viable commercial market for such provision. As the potential is unknown, this is represented in the diagram by a question mark.

The upper left-hand box is where organizations can expect to achieve immediate impact – quick wins – by developing e-learning that is particularly recognizable and relevant to them, but still relatively cheap and easy to develop (like the cash cow). I always recommend this as a good place to start for organizations new to e-learning, as it should be high- (and quick-) impact and low-risk. This is represented in the diagram as a star. Everyone needs more stars.

The upper right-hand box depicts the ideal e-learning solution, bespoke to the organization and enabling real skill development. Needless to say, it is still extremely rare. This is shown in the diagram as a 'Holy Grail', an almost unobtainable, almost legendary, goal.

The main lesson of Figure 2.5 is that the right kind of e-learning *can* impact on skill development, attainment of competence, behaviour change and performance improvement. It is a question of understanding what kind of e-learning should be deployed. Allied to the three component parts and five models discussed in Chapter 1, the Impact Matrix helps organizations understand the many different faces of e-learning and how they can work for them. It is thus an invaluable tool for winning support for e-learning, and ensuring that it meets expectations.

The Impact Matrix can form the basis of a workshop or discussion seeking to broaden colleagues' appreciation of how e-learning works and what it can achieve (indeed, I have used it extensively in this way, with corporate clients and in public workshops). It can offer a lead-in to raising some of the theory in Chapter 1 about the component parts of e-learning and the different models. The matrix helps show that e-learning has a wide range of potential applications in any organization.

ORGANIZATION DEVELOPMENT STRATEGIES

We have seen how e-learning helps underpin, and further enhances, the general concepts of learner-centred learning, developing a learning culture and building a learning organization. Now let's consider how e-learning contributes to various human resources (HR) and organization development (OD) strategies.

Table 2.3 shows the role of e-learning in relation to some of the more common OD strategies. In addition, e-learning can help introduce, promote and sustain initiatives involving psychometrics, emotional intelligence, Neuro-Linguistic Programming, development centres, team building, accelerated learning, experiential learning and many others.

Adjacent to, or overlapping with, OD strategies are strategies linked to quality initiatives such as ISO9000 (and other international standards), Balanced Scorecard, Six Sigma and others. E-learning can also help underpin and further enhance these.

And, of course, e-learning fits into broader e-strategies, the range of initiatives whereby digital technology may be used to leverage greater value for organizations, especially through the use of relational databases, corporate networks, intranets and the web. These could include e-commerce, e-recruitment, e-communications, e-HR and e-just-about-anything. E-learning has great capacity to support other strategies, and should be advocated and developed in this sympathetic way.

Table 2.3 Organization development (OD) strategies

OD strategy	?	Role of e-learning
corporate university	✓	e-learning can provide a virtual university, a portal for information and for registering for courses, online learning sources (model 3), online courses (model 1), and integrated online and offline learning (model 2)
knowledge management	✓	model 3 – self-managed e-learning – and knowledge management are virtually the same thing, at least in terms of learning
talent management	✓	important aspects of talent management are about development and retention of key talent; this is where e-learning comes in
performance management	✓	e-learning can answer many development needs identified in performance management, and e-portfolios can record them
learning centre(s)	✓	learning centres often include online resources and courses, and organizations can also create virtual learning centres
leadership and management development	✓	increasingly, managers expect e-learning to be part of the mix in their development
continuous professional development	✓	model 3 portals can provide resources, progression paths and record keeping such as e-portfolios
classroom-based learning	✗	digital technology can support the classroom, but, as we discussed in Chapter 1, this is not really e-learning
coaching and mentoring	✗	coaches and mentors can communicate with learners via digital devices, but this does not fundamentally change what they do
work-based learning	✓	model 5, EPS

TAKING THE LEAD

Somebody has to take the lead in promoting the concepts in this chapter and advocating e-learning, and in most organizations that needs to be the learning and development professionals. Here are some of the behaviours that characterize that leadership role.

- *Asking questions*: asking managers what their aims are and how e-learning can help fulfil those aims. (Also, taking time to reflect and ask questions of yourself; see the checklist at the end of Chapter 3.)

- *Taking a user-centred approach*: whether it's the customer-centred approach of making sure e-learning meets the organization's needs, or the learner-centred approach of designing e-learning to meet learners' needs – and there needn't be any contradiction between these – you should always look at things from the user's perspective.

- *Looking before you leap*: e-learning is often much faster to roll out than traditional training, which means you have less time to make changes to accommodate unexpected reactions to the learning. This in turn highlights the need for greater thinking and planning before launch.

- *Linking strategy, or project plans, to action*: only producing documents that have meaning for other people, and can be put to practical use.

- *Gathering support*: taking account of all stakeholders, and involving them in the process of introducing e-learning.

- *Measuring value*: subjecting e-learning to rigorous scrutiny – how does it add value? Using evaluation tools, such as those discussed in Chapter 6, to measure e-learning's contribution to fulfilling organizational strategy.

If you work in this way, you should be able to carry the organization with you.

WHEN E-LEARNING IS NOT APPROPRIATE

Nevertheless, there are still circumstances where e-learning is not appropriate. There are three groups of circumstances:

- *Circumstance 1.* Where face-to-face involvement is necessary: e-learning can provide limited audio-visual contact using webcams, microphones and speakers or headsets, but while this can be a good substitute for live contact, it can never match it.

- *Circumstance 2.* When it is necessary to actually be *in situ*, in the workplace: again, e-learning can provide a good substitute using images, videos and especially simulations, but it can never match the real experience. EPS may be an exception to this rule.

- *Circumstance 3.* When learners need to be exposed to a new situation or environment: e-learning can offer a virtual model, but not the real experience. There are pros and cons to this, but sometimes the real experience is necessary, and no off-the-job technique will serve.

These circumstances show once again why e-learning, as an approach, can never be the sole type of learning, but should complement face-to-face and work-based approaches. (Note that these approaches are not mutually exclusive, but overlap. As we have seen, there can be e-learning applications in the workplace, such as EPS, and e-learning applications that blend with face-to-face methods, typified by model 2.)

If we take the prime consideration of effectiveness in meeting learning needs, then if it is essential for the learner to have close personal contact with a coach, manager or trainer, e-learning is not appropriate. If it is essential for the learner to be in the workplace, at work, to learn how to complete a task, then e-learning is not appropriate. If it is essential for the learner to actually experience something new, then again e-learning is not appropriate. E-learning is invaluable, but it is not a panacea.

Sometimes you may encounter people in an organization who want to implement e-learning for the wrong reasons. You should be wary of some of these more common types.

- *Technophiles*, who are excited by the technology and just want to try it out for themselves. Sometimes in an organization you get a cluster of such people, who leave everybody else behind and dismiss as Luddites those who question what they're doing.

- *'Me too-ers'*, who think they should be doing it because everybody else seems to be. This can be a powerful pressure when the 'me too-ers' are senior managers concerned that their competitors are implementing e-learning and they aren't.

- *Cost-cutters*, who believe e-learning is a cheap alternative – as indeed it can be. Having a good-value proposition is one thing, and cutting costs may be a legitimate strategy, but doing training on the cheap rarely works. There is also the danger that learners will think they are being offered a cheap, low-quality option and get the message that they are undervalued. If cutting costs is the sole rationale for e-learning, it had better be a darned well thought through rationale.

- *Quick-fixers*, who are sceptical about e-learning but fob off its advocates by using it for one-offs, or for routine training issues that could easily (and perhaps more effectively) be addressed by other means. These are e-learning tacticians, doomed to miss the real strategic benefits of e-learning.

- *CV-builders*, who want to get involved because it's good for their career, rather than good for their organization. If they achieve effective e-learning, they do so by accident rather than design.

Such people may sometimes be allies in advocating e-learning, but at some point their agenda will diverge from yours. If you have already recognized their motivations, you will be better placed to ensure they do not divert or subvert your e-learning agenda.

In Chapters 1 and 2 we have established the nature and scope of e-learning. We have considered how organizations need to change their thinking, and what learning and development professionals can do to facilitate this change. In the following chapters we turn our attention to the practical applications of this thinking, through the development and implementation of e-learning strategy. None of this may be omitted. Any organization that is serious about implementing e-learning will have to give due attention to the development of an e-learning strategy; to understanding the digital technologies, how they relate to each other, and the role of the vendors who purvey them; to understanding how to design e-learning and adopting a coherent and consistent design approach; and to evaluating the impact of e-learning on the organization, and measuring results.

Illustrative project

I had to make a business case for e-learning. Doing nothing wasn't an option, as we could see how influenced our employees were by digital technology, so senior management were keen to see the arguments for what exactly we should do. I didn't have to sell e-learning with a shopping list of benefits; instead, I needed to show how it could work for us.

I started by describing how e-learning could make our people take more responsibility for their own learning, as it is a process they manage themselves, rather than looking to a tutor as an all-knowing expert. I argued for a very participative sort of e-learning, closely linking the theory to what people actually do in their jobs. And I showed how we could design e-learning to tie in with the key business programmes we operate in our stores, such as customer care, product positioning and keeping stores clean. Basically, I made the case that e-learning would help people do their jobs better, and would help us achieve our targets.

Senior management liked what I had to say, and agreed in principle, but they wanted to see more detail before making any commitment, so they asked me to write a strategy for e-learning and to devise some measures to test whether it actually worked.

SUMMARY OF KEY POINTS

1. E-learning can play a major role in making learning more learner centred, developing a learning culture, building a learning organization and empowering learners.

2. In the digital age it is impossible to ignore e-learning. Every organization will need to develop e-learning in response to employee and other stakeholder expectations.

3. E-learning has many benefits and various capabilities in different contexts. You need to work out what are the best benefits for your organization.

4. E-learning can offer something to suit every learning style preference, and may be the best option for some learning styles.

5. There are five criteria to consider when choosing an e-learning approach. In sequence, these are learning needs, learner style preferences, cost, time and value-add.

6. When advocating e-learning, you need to develop your influencing skills, master change management and aim to achieve a paradigm shift in your organization.

7. The Impact Matrix can help with the advocacy of e-learning in your organization, and in particular can demonstrate what sort of impact different kinds of e-learning will be likely to have.

8. E-learning can complement and support almost any organization development initiative.

9. There are three sets of circumstances when e-learning is not appropriate: where face-to-face involvement is necessary, when the learner actually has to be in the workplace and when the learner has to be exposed to something new. There are also some people who support e-learning for the wrong reasons.

3

E-learning strategy: development

This chapter examines the notion of 'strategy' and clarifies what we mean in the context of e-learning. It explores what you need to do when devising and developing an e-learning strategy, including aligning it with your business strategy and learning and development strategy. Our Virtual Round Table reconvenes to advise on current trends in e-learning. I provide guidance on project planning and quality assurance, introduce consideration of some wider issues and give a personal checklist of questions to ask yourself.

WHAT 'STRATEGY' IS NOT

Let me start by making clear what I do not mean. I need to do this because the popular conception of strategy is wrong. A typical definition is that provided by Wikipedia: 'a strategy is a long term plan of action designed to achieve a particular goal'. Every part of that statement is wrong. For a start, you can have a short-term or medium-term strategy, not just one for the long term. A strategy, as I shall explain, is not the same thing as a plan, far less a 'plan of action'; and it need not be restricted to just one particular goal.

People have all sorts of other prejudices about strategy, which we shall deal with as they arise, but rather than elaborate on them now, let's move on to what I really do mean.

WHAT I MEAN BY 'STRATEGY'

Strategy is one of the most-discussed topics in business. There are many books and learned articles on the subject, and there are many high-level consultants who specialize in business strategy. Perhaps foremost among them is the Harvard Business School professor Michael Porter, whom many credit with inventing the entire discipline. Porter has certainly conceived many tools helpful in understanding and promoting strategy, and has articulated a philosophy of how organizations – and even entire nations – can develop a competitive strategy to obtain lasting competitive advantage.

Porter supplies us with our starting point: 'sound strategy starts with having the right goal'. In this chapter we shall try to establish what e-learning can achieve for your organization, and set our goals accordingly.

Porter also supplies us with a particularly apposite observation, given our field of inquiry, which is that 'the underlying principles of strategy are enduring, regardless of technology'. As we delve deeper into the arcane world of digital technology, we will do well to remember this lesson.

There are many different schools of thought about how to define, determine and manage your strategy. We shall not debate the merits of the different schools, but we shall draw upon the thinking that best seems to serve our needs, which is sometimes characterized as the resource-based school. One of its foremost advocates is John Kay, and we shall draw heavily upon his ideas. Kay asserts that 'strategy begins with an understanding of what [your] distinctive capabilities are'. By this, he means that to get anywhere you need to recognize what you are capable of, as an organization, rather than follow an attractive but inappropriate vision. This chimes with what Porter says about 'the *right* goal'. We need to apply this sort of thinking to e-learning.

This thinking stands in contrast to theories of strategy based on the personal qualities and decisive interventions of heroic individuals, effectively reducing successful strategy to a quest for heroes. And it stands in contrast to vision-based strategies, the extreme versions of which advocate setting sky-high goals in order to achieve miraculous results. Occasionally this approach does indeed yield miraculous results, but more often it leads to underperformance, disillusion and demoralization. In my experience, this is particularly true of learning initiatives when over-ambitious outcomes are eagerly expected – and e-learning has had more than its share of these.

The central proposition of this book is that to implement successful e-learning you need to have a coherent e-learning strategy that is right for your organization, and you need to follow it through. In this chapter and the next three chapters, we will consider what you need to do to develop that strategy (this chapter); what you need to know about, and do with, e-learning suppliers and technology resources (Chapter 4); what you need to take account of in designing e-learning (Chapter 5); and how you should measure e-learning and aim to achieve the results you need (Chapter 6). These are the four main areas that require your attention if you are to implement successful e-learning. Their interrelationship harks back to the three components of e-learning:

- Strategy development is about getting the content of your e-learning right, both in the sense of being appropriate for the learner and in contributing to organizational aims.

- The suppliers and resources provide the technology, so managing them is about getting the technology component right.

- E-learning design is about providing the third component of e-learning.

- The final part of our strategy, evaluation, is about bringing together the three components.

WHY YOU NEED AN E-LEARNING STRATEGY

You need an e-learning strategy for the same reason that you need a learning and development strategy, and that your organization needs an overall business strategy, and probably a number of other strategies. It is a truism that if you don't know where you're going, you won't know when you've got there. However, in the past this consideration led organizations to develop detailed plans for one, two, three or five years or more. Such planning proved inflexible and unrealistic. As things change ever more rapidly in the modern world, the idea of meticulously planning what your organization will be doing in several years' time is widely regarded as unfeasible, if not downright absurd. In five years' time your products and services may have completely changed, most or all of your staff may have moved on, your competitors may have changed (or you may have merged with them), your markets may have been transformed by external events you cannot anticipate, and your organization itself may no longer exist, at least in its current form. And as regards learning, you can take it as certain that learning needs in your organization will have changed beyond all recognition.

The use of strategy, rather than planning, at a corporate level reflects this state of flux and the accompanying need to be more flexible. A strategy is an appreciation of your potential, a vision, a description of the general approach you aim to take, and a statement of values underpinning this approach – a set of guidelines rather than a detailed blueprint. Rather than a fixed compass, it is adapted as your circumstances and resources change, so that your course remains within your scope.

According to John Kay, 'each firm is characterized by its own individual collection of resources', therefore 'the essential strategic question for any firm is how well its capabilities match its activities'. Ultimately, 'the strategy of the firm is the match between its internal capabilities and its external relationships'. In short, it's about using your distinctive capabilities to achieve competitive advantage. Learning and development professionals who work for public or charitable bodies may prefer to adapt this perspective to consider how their distinctive capabilities may be harnessed to achieve public or social policy goals.

The same principles may be applied to setting and pursuing strategy *within* the organization, in specific functions such as learning and development, or even in relation to specific approaches such as e-learning. You need to assess and develop your resources (see Chapter 4), build your capability in e-learning (see Chapter 5) and then match that to the learning needs of your employees and the organization as a whole (see Chapter 6). This process is summarized in Figure 3.1.

If you are introducing e-learning, you will need a strategy to demonstrate and ensure that it is consistent with the learning and development strategy, and with the corporate strategy as a whole. This strategic alignment should enable you to link your e-learning goals and outcomes to the

assess/develop
resources

build
capability

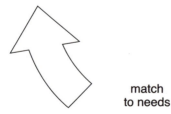

match
to needs

Figure 3.1 Strategy development cycle

organization's vision, mission, values, performance indicators and specific objectives, and thence show the value of e-learning.

You cannot commit to e-learning without developing a strategy. As Don Morrison puts it, 'without a robust, business-driven strategy to guide implementation and delivery, e-learning is bound to fail'.

The other reason you need an e-learning strategy is tactical, if you'll pardon the paradox. Because e-learning is relatively new, and still so widely misunderstood, disseminating an e-learning strategy can play a vital part in helping everyone in the organization reach a better understanding of what e-learning is and what it means. In practical terms this suggests that any strategy document you produce should include explicit statements of some of the points from the preceding chapters.

I believe strongly that you need not just a strategy but an explicit strategy. In view of the widespread confusion around e-learning, most organizations need a written strategy document that is widely distributed, read and understood. Depending on your situation, you may even need more than one document – perhaps variations for different business divisions, or an introductory document prior to the main one, or tailored versions for different groups of employees or other stakeholders. Producing these takes time and preparation, but repays that effort in the long run. Too many people plunge straight into e-learning without enough thought in advance – the 'fire, aim, ready' school – and this is an impatience we must all try to guard against.

WHERE TO START

You should start to examine the issue of strategy development from the outside and work in. You need to take account of the context in which you are working, and that means not just your organizational circumstances but your business situation, the market conditions and the overall socio-economic environment. Your examination should include taking an overview of what is happening in the world of learning and development generally, not just e-learning.

A useful tool to aid this process is PEST analysis. PEST stands for Political, Economic, Social and Technological analysis, and categorizes the factors you need to consider.

Political factors may be especially important for public bodies, or community organizations reliant upon public funding, or industries that are heavily regulated or subject to public scrutiny, but increasingly these days that could mean almost any organization. One example that impacts on e-learning is the range of regulations and compliance issues affecting the financial services sector. These issues mean that organizations such as banks and insurance companies have an obligation to measure and report training activity, and no system does this more efficiently than e-learning, as web-based learning activity can be tracked and recorded.

Economic factors may dictate what you can afford to invest in e-learning, the number of people you are likely to have to develop, or other constraints on what you can do. If you are forced to find a more cost-effective solution, e-learning could provide it.

Social factors may determine your priorities, if there are issues of overriding concern to your stakeholders. Examples of these might be ecological concerns, or perhaps health and safety issues. These could dictate your subject agenda, or could constrain what you can do if, for example, employees are already deemed to be spending too much time in front of their monitors.

Technological factors should be an obvious set of considerations when looking at e-learning, but perhaps the most fundamental issues to include at this stage are the technological capacity of your organization, its network size and infrastructure, and any limitations of the terminals available to end users, such as lack of sound cards or restrictions of plugins. You need to be sure that your organization, including its people, is ready for whatever technology-based solution you intend to offer it.

Whether you classify the various issues as political, economic, social or technological is not important, and you may have noticed that some of the examples cited could fit more than one category. What *is* important is that this analysis tool helps you tease out all the issues, so that you can begin to focus in, and arrive at answers that take account of the wider issues. A variant of PEST analysis adds legal and environmental issues as separate categories for consideration, yielding the extended acronym PESTLE.

This book can contribute to your PEST, or PESTLE, analysis by offering an overview of current trends in e-learning.

Virtual Round Table: Part 3

I asked each of our international experts to consider what the main trends in e-learning are at the moment.

Elena Tikhomirova believes, 'Web 2.0 and gaming technologies are the most interesting and trendy at the moment. My personal belief is that situational (game-based) learning will be the main vector of e-learning development in the future. Overloaded with information, people need learning that will help them to resolve their problems at the moment and place of need.'

The same sense of immediacy led Allison Rossett to rather different conclusions. Allison identifies the use of handheld devices in remote locations as a vital business tool, including for learning. 'Obviously, e-learning has grown to be more than lessons and tutorials,' she observes, citing the example of a saleswoman constantly on the move who uses the web to update herself, and 'when a customer stumps her with a question, she turns to her personal digital assistant for access to her corporate portal'.

Personalization is a key theme for Marius Meyer, who cautions, 'One-size-fits-all technology does not work. A high level of customization according to the needs of the target market and the particular organization is needed to ensure that the system is relevant in the application environment.'

Nigel Paine takes that one step further and, in an echo of Elena's comments, emphasizes the greater participation of learners, to the extent that they themselves provide an increasing proportion of learning content. He describes the trend as 'towards more non-linear multi-media materials; use of user-generated content; incorporating the formal content in informal learning environments; learning in bits; materials from disparate sources; non-inclusive material that sends the learner to alternative sources and treats the learner more as an adult able to discriminate between different materials from different places with different levels of authenticity'.

Part of Nigel's vision is taken up with enthusiasm by Serge Ravet. Serge forecasts 'a shift from formal to informal learning. Ninety per cent of what we learn is informal, but 90 per cent of our effort goes into formal learning, so technology will increasingly focus on the informal'.

A closing note of caution comes from Martyn Sloman, who warns that, whatever the latest development, 'expectations always exceed reality'. However, 'when the circus leaves town, we're always a bit further forward'.

STRATEGIC ALIGNMENT

Some people are suspicious of the term 'strategic', perhaps because they hear others abuse it, and realize that sometimes it is meant just as a grand-sounding substitute word for 'important'. The two are not really the same. Nor is it true that strategy is just for senior management; senior managers may have the final say in setting strategy, but strategy, both in development and in action, is for everyone. Others feel that strategy is theoretical, and theory is anti-practice. Again, this is understandable if the strategy or theory doesn't appear to relate to your reality. But theory and practice should be interrelated, each informing the other, and strategy is what binds them together.

Applying this thinking, if we have a theory about what e-learning should contribute, and what it should achieve for the organization, then we should use this theory to devise a strategy, which is an approach and guidelines if not quite a detailed plan. This strategy should then be converted into action as the e-learning is implemented, and should serve as a reference point, with constant checks that the e-learning is 'on-strategy'. This is significant in recording outcomes and measuring results, as we shall see later.

Let's take an illustration of this. A company is looking for ways to get its geographically spread workplaces to cooperate more, in the belief that better cooperation will yield synergies, savings and improvements for the business. The learning and development function agrees to work towards this by bringing together staff from different locations for various learning initiatives. One of these is an e-learning programme, so the model chosen is integrated online and offline learning (our model 2), with milestone face-to-face workshops and the online part including live synchronous tutorial meetings, while participants are also encouraged to work together in a collaborative wiki (see the next chapter). At periodic reviews, learning and development professionals, working with line managers in each of the locations, check that learners from different locations are actually working together and not simply meeting their individual objectives for the programme.

This illustration shows strategic alignment in practice. In any organization there are overlapping layers of strategy: overall corporate strategy; strategic business units; functional strategies that could encompass e-learning, such as learning and development or general HR strategy, ICT or e-business strategy, or perhaps a knowledge management strategy; and still more specialized strategies within them, which is where e-learning sits (see Figure 3.2).

There are some simple things you can make certain each strategy shares in common, to help ensure strategic alignment. The statements should be written in the same language style, adopting common phraseology; goals of 'subsidiary' strategies should be consistent with the goals of the 'higher' strategies; the values or principles should be the same; the same communication channels should be used to disseminate the

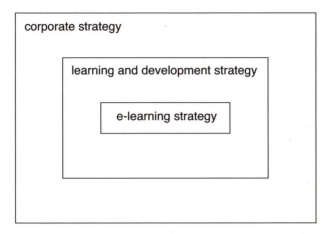

Figure 3.2 Strategy alignment

strategy; and in some instances the same people can be responsible for implementation.

In 2008 the CIPD published research outcomes on aligning learning to the needs of the organization, citing Michael Porter on the importance of this to ensure fit, linkage or integration of strategy and action. The lessons are valuable for e-learning too. The CIPD found that there are three aspects to strategic alignment:

1. clarifying how learning can contribute to strategic priorities;

2. delivering and evaluating cost-effective and aligned learning processes;

3. maintaining ongoing alignment.

Substitute e-learning for learning in aspects 1 and 2, and we have a useful guide to ensuring that e-learning is aligned with the wider strategic needs of the organization. Getting alignment right is about clarifying expectations, making sure these are consistent for the different levels of strategy, and constantly checking that this fit is maintained.

PROJECT PLANNING

We have distinguished a strategy from a plan, but that is not to say that strategy does not involve any planning. Within the overall scope of a strategy, plans have to be made and carried out, such as a plan to generate e-learning design capability, or a small-scale e-learning implementation, or even the initiating and rolling out of an e-learning course for hundreds of staff over a period of perhaps a year or more. This falls within the scope of project planning, and if your organization has an established approach to project planning, then that is what you should use for e-learning too.

It would be futile to offer a unique planning model as though e-learning is unique, yet some vendors propose exactly that. Some advocate planning for different phases of e-learning implementation, distinguishing the design or build phase from the delivery phase. If this sounds familiar, it should; these are two (but just two) of the four stages of the standard training cycle (see Figure 1.2 in Chapter 1).

I recommend using this training cycle as the basis of your project planning for e-learning, for consistency with other learning and development activities, and to ensure you are considering all aspects of an e-learning implementation. Any strategic plan to implement an e-learning programme should thus address the following four steps:

- *Step 1: identifying and analysing learning needs*. This first step may include collation and study of information from individual performance reviews, employee surveys, managers' reports, suggestion schemes, business reviews, customer feedback and other sources, including, not least, the outcomes of step 4 (below) for previous implementations. Your analysis should seek to identify common issues, patterns and trends, and issues of major urgency or importance.

- *Step 2: planning and preparation of the e-learning*. This step may include selecting the people who will undertake the learning, selecting the technologies and other resources to use, selecting any vendors, determining a timescale, perhaps producing a project plan in your organization's preferred format (a GANTT chart? critical path analysis and a network diagram?) or using your organization's preferred project management software, designing and testing the e-learning, and completing all the last-minute preparations such as issuing joining instructions.

- *Step 3: delivery of the e-learning*. This step should, I hope, be self-explanatory: actually running the programme. Aspects include the support arrangements (tutors, mentors, the role of managers, peer support from other learners) and a feedback loop to check that pre-designed learning components, such as online course content, are actually delivering what they are supposed to do. This leads us into step 4.

- *Step 4: assessment, evaluation and review of the e-learning.* We shall consider in detail in Chapter 6 what is involved in this step. For the moment, it is sufficient to observe that we need to consider how learners perform against the learning objectives, and we need to consider how the e-learning performs against the objectives the organization sets for it.

A more general way of describing these four steps would be in accordance with general planning principles. First you have to gather and analyse your information, then you have to produce a plan, then you have to implement the plan and finally you have to review what has happened, with a view to future planning needs. Perhaps it should not be surprising that a general planning cycle is actually remarkably similar to the training cycle.

You may use any or all of the familiar planning tools and techniques that you probably already apply to other learning and development work – or other business activities, such as SWOT analysis, which is especially useful for step 1. You can assess the strengths, weaknesses, opportunities and threats for an employee, workgroup, division or entire organization, in relation to the subject, skills or business issue under consideration.

Project plans also need to take account of all the people who have interests in the project. Identifying all the stakeholders, considering their interests and winning their commitment represents a people-centred way of taking account of all aspects of the project. For e-learning, the stakeholders will include all the prospective learners; their (internal and external) customers and suppliers (in other words, everyone in the value chain); their managers, immediate colleagues and subordinates (everyone close to them in the organizational structure); everyone involved in providing the e-learning; and anyone else you feel should be affected or interested in any way.

Project plans are about implementing strategy, about turning vision and values into objectives and measures of success, such as key performance indicators, about transforming ideas into reality. They are about 'getting down to brass tacks', while still retaining enough detachment to keep questioning what you are doing.

STRATEGIC QUESTIONS IN E-LEARNING

The primary questions about e-learning we need to answer are centred round what it is and why we need it. That's why we began this book with chapters on understanding e-learning and advocacy of e-learning.

The secondary questions we need to ask are about our organization and its distinctive capabilities. By this I mean both the capability of the organization's people to learn, and the capability of the learning and development function and its partners to provide e-learning.

The tertiary questions are about how you go about devising and implementing an e-learning strategy, what factors you need to consider and whom you need to involve. These include the vital consideration of aligning e-learning strategy to learning and development and corporate strategies. All the issues raised in this and the following chapters must be considered.

Lastly, there are questions you need to ask yourself. A checklist of these is provided at the end of this chapter.

You can constantly interrogate everything you do by using the classic 5WH model. Before you plan or do anything, ask all the relevant questions of it: *who, what, where, when, why* and *how*.

For example, consider *who* the learning is for, and who will provide the e-learning; who will design the learning environment, who will author the learning content, who will manage and administer it, who will provide tuition, whom learners will interact with, etc.

What is to be learned, and what exactly will the e-learning comprise? What are the objectives?

Where will the e-learning be hosted, where will it be administered and, most important of all, where will the learners learn (in the workplace? in learning centres? at home?)?

When will the various steps of the e-learning project be implemented? (What is the timetable?) When will learners learn? (Hopefully, whenever they want, but what restrictions are there, and when – by what deadline – must their learning be completed?)

Why is this being done by e-learning?

How will the e-learning work? What will learners do; how will they learn?

These are just examples. You can pose some or all of these questions about every step along the way.

THE ESSENTIAL ELEMENTS OF AN E-LEARNING STRATEGY STATEMENT

The first thing an e-learning strategy document needs to do is clarify what you mean by e-learning, so that everyone in the organization has a common approach. This should draw upon the information in Chapter 1 and contextualize it for your particular situation.

Second, the strategy document needs to include a clear statement of aims and objectives, recognizably linked to more general aims and objectives for learning and development, and to those of the organization as a whole. Your statement should be redolent of your corporate values and culture, and should be written in the corporate style and language.

Third, the strategy document needs to provide a framework for action plans, project work, quality assurance and other initiatives. It needs to provide guidance to everyone involved in e-learning.

Fourth, it needs to consider the resourcing of e-learning, and the partners involved in this. These will include all the learners who may use e-learning, and their managers; senior management, who will wish to influence e-learning; your ICT function, whose technical expertise will be invaluable, and who will ensure that what you do is consistent with your ICT strategy; your knowledge management function, if you have one; potentially interested parties from the wider community, such as shareholders, customers, families of employees, and others; and, last but by no means least, external suppliers (see Chapter 4).

Fifth, it needs to consider which model or models you will deploy (see Chapter 1), how you will approach e-learning, and the design principles you will follow (see Chapter 5).

Finally, it needs to show how you will evaluate e-learning. Here the same principles apply as in evaluating any kind of learning. Evaluation will be discussed in greater detail in Chapter 6.

Table 3.1 gives a visual representation of the six essential elements of an e-learning strategy document. In all of them, the document should seek to *persuade*.

Table 3.1 Elements of an e-learning strategy

	Element	*Purpose*
1.	definition of e-learning	shared understanding
2.	aims and objectives	shared vision
3.	planning framework	shared way of working
4.	resources and partners	who and what is involved
5.	models of e-learning	common approach and design
6.	evaluation approach	how results will be measured

VENDOR DISTRACTIONS AND DIVERSIONS

The role of vendors in your strategy development can be very significant. It can be a touchstone of the value of a vendor, as those who are not interested in getting involved, when asked, betray a lack of interest in anything other than selling their products to you.

The sharper vendors will see the opportunity to influence your strategy and should welcome involvement, but you need to be careful not to let them take over. A recurring problem for learning and development professionals is that software vendors tend to be better informed about techie issues and the latest industry fads, and do not always share that information in the most helpful way. You need to steer them towards providing technical expertise supportively, while allowing learning and development considerations to lead.

Vendors may try to dissuade you from a particular course of action on the grounds that they do not believe it will work. They could be right, or they could be wary of the limitations of their software (as opposed, perhaps, to that of their competitors), or they could be trying to keep their offer centre stage at the expense of whatever else may be best for you. It always pays to listen to criticism, but if a vendor claims that an approach does not work, ask them for references – other clients you can talk to, to establish whether that is true. Better still, do your own research: find others who have adopted your preferred approach and see whether it worked for them (and if not, why not; it could still work for you).

Vendors will always look for opportunities to play with the technology. Often, the main way they carry out their product development is at their clients' expense. They may ask you to fund additional functionality for their product on the grounds that it is essential for your project, but really so that they can develop the capability for their other clients. It may indeed be essential for you, but in these circumstances you should at most contribute just part of the development cost (or share in the profits of the development).

On the whole, it helps to get vendors on board, as long as you maintain the perspective that they do not always have your best interests at heart. The next chapter will look in more detail at how to get the most from your vendor relationships.

QUALITY-ASSURING E-LEARNING

As you develop your e-learning strategy you need to consider how you will evaluate it. This is the subject of Chapter 6, but needs to be raised at this stage as it is inextricably linked with strategy development. One way of managing or, if you prefer, assuring the quality of e-learning is to consider four strategic dimensions of e-learning: strategy setting, technology and resources, infrastructure, and results (see Figure 3.3).

The following is a list of statements for each of these dimensions, which collectively may form the basis of a quality management system.

Strategy setting

1. Your organization has an explicit e-learning strategy.

2. Goals, values and commitment are expressed in the e-learning strategy.

3. Your e-learning strategy is informed by learning needs analyses.

4. Your e-learning strategy is informed by all relevant industry, professional and statutory requirements and recommendations.

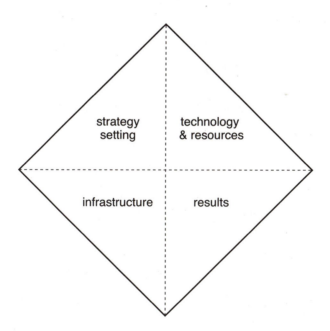

Figure 3.3 Quality assurance model

Technology and resources

1. The appropriate ICT infrastructure is maintained.

2. All learning and development staff are suitably trained and qualified.

3. Budgets are in place to sustain ongoing e-learning.

4. ICT support is in place, especially for end users (learners).

5. Learners have access to the best possible learning resources.

6. Your organization maintains a database of all its e-learning provision, and relevant e-learning provision by suppliers and partners.

Infrastructure

1. Reporting mechanisms are in place for e-learning, including regular monitoring and review of e-learning's effectiveness.

2. Your organization has a coordinated approach to e-learning, with central control of implementation of the e-learning strategy.

3. Your organization maintains records of all its e-learning activities.

4. Your organization conducts regular assessments to match business needs with e-learning provision.

5. Your organization links e-learning to its performance management system.

Results

1. Where appropriate, online learning should be linked to practical experience, to transfer learning to the workplace.

2. E-learning is consistently at an appropriate level to meet learning needs identified throughout the organization.

3. E-learning provision fulfils the goals of the e-learning strategy.

4. E-learning is regularly reviewed to ensure it meets industry and/or national standards.

5. You can show that e-learning provision impacts positively on product quality and customer service.

6. You can show that e-learning provision saves on expenditure, increases revenue, and/or increases profit.

The people responsible for implementing e-learning in your organization need to expand each of these statements to reflect the specific circumstances of your particular e-learning initiatives, devise means to generate evidence against each statement, and record performance to demonstrate quality. We shall return to these issues in Chapter 6.

QUESTIONS TO ASK YOURSELF

Finally, here is a checklist of questions to ask yourself when formulating your e-learning strategy:

1. What are the key ways in which e-learning can benefit my organization?
2. What specific learning and development would be better delivered by e-learning?
3. What is the best model (or models) for e-learning in my organization?
4. What are the critical success factors for e-learning in my organization?
5. How can I best make the case for e-learning in my organization?
6. Can I show that e-learning goals meet organizational goals?
7. What steps do I need to take to get key influencers to support e-learning?
8. What suppliers do we need?
9. How do I get the most from these suppliers?
10. What steps do I need to take to ensure that learners engage with e-learning?

If you can give a well-thought-through answer to each of these questions, then you will have the makings of a coherent strategy and you should be well on the way to implementing successful e-learning.

Illustrative project

Writing an e-learning strategy wasn't as hard as I thought. In fact, it helped me see the learning and development strategy in a whole new light. Making sure the strategies fitted together was vital, and of course it had to make sense in terms of our business strategy too. I looked at the things we seem to do well and the things I thought we could do better, and tried to map out a path for e-learning that would support those. For example, we try to get people to take responsibility for their own work areas, and taking responsibility for the parallel parts of e-learning could implicitly encourage that.

Another critical part of the strategy was to show how we would plan specific courses, giving guidance to those who would create and run the courses, and managers who would be looking to direct their staff to them. I built in some checkpoints to make sure our courses would be consistent and would be planned to work.

Lastly, I made sure the strategy offered a vision – a powerful sense of where e-learning could take us, which I hoped would help get everyone in the company on board.

SUMMARY OF KEY POINTS

1. Strategy is about linking your distinctive capabilities to achievable goals; it is more flexible than long-term planning, and forms a bridge between theory and practice.

2. Your e-learning strategy should be governed by the same principles as other strategies in your organization, and should be aligned to these other strategies, especially your learning and development strategy and your overall business strategy. You should start by looking at the broader context before narrowing your focus.

3. You need an explicit e-learning strategy statement because of the widespread confusion about e-learning.

4. Your e-learning strategy document should include clarification of what you mean by e-learning; aims and objectives; a framework for planning, and guidance to everyone involved; consideration of resources and partners; your models, approach and design principles; and how you will evaluate e-learning.

5. More detailed planning of e-learning initiatives should be based on the standard training and development cycle, and on the standard approach to planning you use in your organization.

6.   You need to involve vendors, as well as all other stakeholders, in your strategy development, while being wary of their distractions and diversions.

7.   You need to prepare to manage the quality of your e-learning via consideration of four dimensions: strategy setting, technology and resources, infrastructure, and results.

8.   You need to constantly ask questions concerning what you are doing.

E-learning strategy: suppliers and resources

This chapter considers the role of technology vendors and the technological resources they offer. It casts a sceptical eye over vendors' use of jargon, and some of the spurious claims vendors make. It looks at e-learning standards and specifications, and the various technology applications on the market, not least virtual learning environments (VLEs) and the more recent growth of participative tools such as wikis and blogs. Lastly, it discusses how to identify, classify, select and manage vendors, and how to manage resources to a budget.

ICT MEETS HR

If you are an HR or learning and development professional, then the chances are you're not a specialist in information and communication technology. There is no shame in that; how much do ICT professionals know about HR? E-learning projects are invariably multidisciplinary, and everyone contributes what they can to make them work, with the important caveat that the learning and development professionals should take the lead. This chapter should confirm the least you need to know to identify and source, and direct and manage, your suppliers and resources.

Frankly, it is not necessary to become a technology expert, or even a technophile, to understand and implement e-learning. What is important is that you recognize what the technology is capable of – or can call upon someone to explain it to you – and can access expertise and technology resources to create the learning applications you want. The perspective you should always maintain is that the technology exists to serve the learning needs – not the other way around.

Erich Fromm said that 'education makes machines which act like men and produces men who act like machines'. This is not how we mean things to happen, and is surely a pitfall that technologists and education-alists alike should seek to avoid.

Technology vendors should not be allowed to mystify e-learning with techie jargon, as they frequently attempt to do. It's like distance learning providers insisting on using publishing jargon all the time, or work-based learning advocates obsessing over the esoterica of different working envi-ronments. Perhaps digital technology is more relevant than these exam-ples, but that should prompt techies to strive to make it more accessible to their clients, not less. In this chapter you will encounter many criti-cisms of technology vendors, and a lot of them come back to this strange insistence on maintaining a language of their own, despite the problems it causes their clients.

The technology is, of course, invaluable. And we can carry criticism of techies too far. ICT professionals may sometimes speak a language so foreign it seems like Martian, but learning and development profession-als can be guilty of this too, with HR jargon that others may regard as almost Venusian. E-learning should seek to bring down to Earth the lan-guages of Venus and Mars.

THE E-LEARNING INDUSTRY

Many find the landscape of e-learning confusing, and the relationship between the various services on offer unclear. There have been many attempts to make sense of it. One example comes from when I undertook consultancy work for Scottish Enterprise in 2001, and I found they had constructed an 'e-learning value chain'. This arranged distinct activities in e-learning into a sequence subdivided into a *supply side*, comprising content creation, web enabling, service development and service man-agement, and a *demand side*, comprising consumption and application. One of the problems with this classification was that it was somewhat contrived and artificial; another was that very few participants in the e-learning industry fitted neatly into just one category. Indeed, educational institutions seemed to straddle the supply and demand sides, which left the value of the model open to question.

In the corporate market, suppliers are seeking to sell to a demand side that includes learning and development professionals, who in turn are supplying an internal market of employees and their managers. Thus, there are people in the industry – e-learning specialists – who can move between the supply and demand sides, as is the case in the more general supply of other learning and development services.

We can describe an e-learning market, although whether an e-learning industry actually exists is open to question, but what is certain is that there are many e-learning vendors, and many of them are very different.

In the late 1990s, universities and colleges began to develop e-learning services, and for a while some of them, sometimes acting in consortia, started to offer online degrees and other services, often setting up separate commercial enterprises to sell them. Most of these have now gone, and the preferred approach of most academic institutions is to integrate e-learning into their mainstream curricula.

Again in the late 1990s, the world's leading publishers all started to get involved in e-learning and invested millions in what they believed would be a major new revenue stream for them. When the expected returns failed to materialize, most of them took fright, and from 2001 onwards began to withdraw from the market. Leading houses such as McGraw-Hill and Pearson abandoned or sold their interests in e-learning services for the corporate market.

Those that provided courses on CD ROM in the 1990s began to migrate their offers to the web, and those that survived this upheaval (including the involvement of the big publishers) gradually consolidated, until this part of the market became dominated by SkillSoft. In the past five years there has also been significant consolidation among platform vendors (see below).

The result is that the e-learning industry, apart from the exceptions cited above, is now full of relatively small vendors, often operating mainly or exclusively in their home market, often aspiring to grow but lacking the scale, the financial resources, the market reach or the intelligence to do so. The fragmentation of the e-learning industry is one reason why it seems so complicated and is so hard to understand. Let's examine these vendors in more detail.

VENDORS

E-learning technology vendors (or suppliers – we use the terms more or less interchangeably, although 'suppliers' is perhaps a broader term, applicable also to internal suppliers) rarely have much expertise in learning, and it is unwise to assume they do. By definition, they are technology experts, rather than learning specialists, and they should be retained to focus on their area of expertise. Unfortunately, e-learning technology vendors sometimes profess expertise in learning that they do not possess, and this is something the buyer should guard against, rather than accept at face value.

Many vendors profess to offer 'e-learning solutions', but what is their true expertise? A good starting point is to identify their core competence and then deduce what other competences they claim that are really just add-ons to broaden their appeal, when in fact others may be better placed to serve your needs. The following is a classification of e-learning suppliers. Most are specialists in just one of these six fields, occasionally two:

- consultants;

- writers/developers;

- generic courseware vendors;

- learning platform, or VLE, providers;

- authoring tools providers;

- providers of specialist software (eg assessment or revision tools, games, simulations, etc).

Core competence is about identifying an organization's distinctive capabilities, as we discussed in the previous chapter, and each e-learning vendor should really have a strategy based on its core competence. Gary Hamel and C K Prahalad describe such competence as 'the patient and persistent accumulation of intellectual capital' (more on intellectual capital in Chapter 6). Unfortunately, many have strategies based on unrealistic aspirations instead, so let's look at what we mean by each of our six categories of vendor and try to identify the core competences of each.

Consultants

The first category, consultants, is a bit of a catch-all, but it should include organizations and people like this author who provide information, advice, coaching and support on e-learning strategy and implementation. It should also include some applied technology experts, and specialists in specific types of e-learning project. It is a self-description many vendors will offer, when in fact they fit more readily in one of the other categories, but it is a necessary category to capture those who do not fit the remaining categories.

Writers/developers

The second category is clearer: writers and developers are the people who author e-learning courses or design other types of e-learning initiative. Generally, it includes those who handle only one part of this process, such as subject-matter experts who contribute content to be adapted, designed or programmed by others. In practice, you are unlikely to come across many external suppliers offering this service, but it is common within organizations or communities that have highly specialized subject experts. Other specialists could include learning designers who can write, edit and shape learning content for an online application but may lack programming expertise or knowledge of the particular systems you are using. Or another subcategory would be programmers who simply adapt courseware and publish it to the web.

Generic courseware vendors

The third category includes companies that offer catalogues of 'off-the-shelf' courses, or standard e-learning packages, such as basic customer service or finance for non-financial managers. There used to be many of these companies, but they have gradually merged until this sector is now very consolidated, and dominated by one US company, SkillSoft, that has acquired its leading competitors, such as Smartforce and Thomson NETg. There are still some other large providers in the market, such as Element K and Ivy Learning Services, along with some that specialize in certain market niches, such as Wide Learning for financial services and BPP for professional exam-driven courses.

Learning platform, or VLE, providers

The fourth category includes all those suppliers that offer comprehensive technology systems for e-learning, rather than learning content or design, commonly identified by the neat but ambiguous metaphor of 'platforms'. The idea is that the content and design are superstructures to be built onto the essential base of the 'platform' (except that they are not really 'essential', but we shall come to that). 'Platform' is a piece of ICT jargon referring to a software framework, including system architecture, operating systems and programming languages. In an e-learning context we have learning platforms, which go by a number of other confusing names, often abbreviated, and sometimes specific to one or other vendor. Perhaps the best-known learning platform is Blackboard, which mainly serves the education sector, but there are countless others, often more focused on the corporate market ('enterprise-wide platforms'), often operating mainly or exclusively in their home country. Current examples would be Saba and SumTotal Systems from the United States, Giunti Labs from Italy, Tata Interactive Systems from India, and Kallidus from the United Kingdom; there are many more. There are also wider enterprise platforms, such as HR platforms, that include a VLE or something akin to it; examples include SAP and Oracle's PeopleSoft.

Authoring tools providers

The fifth category comprises vendors of relatively simple software packages that enable users to create e-learning themselves without the need for any programmers or software developers. Most learning platforms include (or can include, at an extra cost) an authoring tool, but there are still many vendors that specialize in offering a stand-alone tool, although they have to work hard to demonstrate to clients that their tool is compatible with the various platforms the client uses, or may use at any point in the future. Authoring tools are often associated with the concept of 'rapid e-learning development', which we shall consider in more detail later. Examples of authoring tools include Lectora, ToolBook and Authorware.

Providers of specialist software

The sixth category is another catch-all, this time for vendors of niche products that defy the other five categories. What they all have in common is that they represent just one part of the e-learning jigsaw, rarely standing alone, but depending on working in conjunction with product offerings in the other categories. These products are often very impressive, but typically do not add significant value to the learning proposition. Vendors in this category are especially inclined to regard their products as world-beating, regardless of how little their enthusiasm is shared by others. The range here is too diverse to attempt a representative list of examples, but it includes vendors of e-assessment software, vendors of systems for creating games and simulations, and those that provide even narrower niche offerings such as animated avatars, 3D panoramic imaging, dynamic mind-maps, and other esoterica.

It is hardly surprising, with such a bewildering array of offers, that vendors tend to claim that they offer a complete e-learning solution. But this claim is not made out of a sense of obligation to customers to clear things up. Instead, it is about securing a bigger market share for the vendor making the claim. And the claim is rarely truthful. I am particularly suspicious of vendors who offer 'end-to-end solutions' (that is, they think they can do everything). Seldom can the ancient warning of *caveat emptor* – buyer beware – have been more apt.

Cynicism infects technology vendors. The most famous vendor of them all, Bill Gates, said, 'Software suppliers are trying to make their software packages more "user-friendly". Their best approach, so far, has been to take all the old brochures and stamp the words "user-friendly" on the cover.'

E-LEARNING STANDARDS AND SPECIFICATIONS

Vendors, and others who should know better, such as some academics, often make a big issue out of e-learning standards (by which, of course, they mean e-learning *technology* standards), and insist on compliance. I have never considered compliance with standards to be particularly important. It often seems like another example of techies trying to baffle learning and development professionals with technical details of limited relevance.

The most frequently cited concept in e-learning standards is SCORM (Sharable Content Object Reference Model): you will often come across questions as to whether an element of e-learning technology is SCORM compliant, but this can be misleading, as SCORM is not itself a standard, and there are different aspects to it. The latest version of SCORM includes an overview and four 'specification books', namely a content aggregation model, run-time environment, sequencing and navigation, and conformance requirements (see Table 4.1).

If all that sounds too complicated, a simple summary is that 'SCORM is a collection of standards and specifications adapted from multiple sources to provide a comprehensive suite of e-learning capabilities that enable interoperability, accessibility and reusability of Web-based learning content.' This is how it is described by its owners: SCORM is a registered trademark of the Advanced Distributed Learning initiative of the US Department of Defense.

SCORM has been around since 2000, and at the time of writing has been through four versions, along the way bringing together standards and specifications from many bodies, including AICC, IMS, IEEE and ARIADNE. At least it seems to be moving in the right direction. It is understandable that the US Department of Defense, the largest military bureaucracy in the world, needs to standardize and codify everything that it works with, particularly for compatibility and as a means of quality-assuring products and services from suppliers. What is less understandable is why the rest of the world needs to follow suit (unless

Table 4.1 Aspects of SCORM (Sharable Content Object Reference Model)

Specification book	Explanation
content aggregation model	defines the metadata used to describe e-learning content, thereby dictating the packaging of e-learning objects
run-time environment	defines how e-learning content and virtual learning environments should communicate
sequencing and navigation	defines the ordering of the elements, and how they link up
conformance requirements	specifies what the requirements are, according to SCORM

they are planning on supplying or partnering the US Department of Defense).

In passing, we should note the difference between compliance and conformance, not least because unscrupulous vendors may conflate them to confuse their clients. Compliance refers to standards, conformance to specifications, which are not the same thing: compliance is the ability to operate in the way defined by a standard, while conformance is the ability to operate in the way defined by a specification. A specification is more of a work-in-progress, while a standard is a more fixed thing. It follows that conforming to a specification is much less useful or meaningful than complying with a standard.

The principles of uniformity and consistency in technology for e-learning *are* important, and that is where standards come in, but there is a tendency to overemphasize them. You do not need to become an expert on SCORM (or any of its contributory standards or specifications – and there are plenty of them) to know what is best for learning, and what makes strategic sense for your organization.

It is better to clarify what you want, and may want, the software to be able to do, and get its supplier to guarantee that it does it. For example, if you want e-learning content to be transferable from one virtual learning environment to another, get the supplier to demonstrate that it can be done and guarantee to engineer it. Some may say the flaw in this plan is that the supplier may go bust. This is certainly a risk, but you can (and should) guard against such a possible calamity via escrow agreements giving you access to the software code in that event, accompanied by a contingency plan to switch to another supplier. And pay attention to *de facto* standards, where something has become 'standardized' simply in the sense that it is very commonly used. The key concept is interoperability; technology has to be compatible with whatever other technology you have or anticipate you may acquire.

Don Morrison, in his 2003 book *E-learning Strategies*, cites a good example of vendors deliberately muddying the waters:

> Vendors will tell you their products are 'AICC compliant'. This only means that they have implemented some of the nine AICC guidelines. Since different vendors can implement different guidelines, AICC compliance does not ensure interoperability.

But don't be bamboozled by vendors evangelizing about standards. Cut through the jargon by getting them to spell out exactly why adherence to a standard is important. Ask questions such as 'What protection does it offer me?', 'What are the risks of not adhering to standards?', 'Why that particular standard?' and 'Is compliance or conformance needed, and what's the difference?' You should soon arrive at the limits of their understanding: for many, it is simply a question of blind faith.

The related issue of reusable learning objects will be addressed later, in our discussion of authoring tools.

To sum up what we have established so far, there is jargon, there are vendors and there are technology standards and specifications. There's more too, but the central question we need to ask is: what does the technology actually do?

WHAT THE TECHNOLOGY DOES

Anyone can build a website – even a technophobe! And you don't need any technical skills such as programming; you don't need to know what HTML is, far less how to write it. Web space is readily available, inexpensive (sometimes free) and easy to populate. Many vendors offer simple design templates where what you see is what you get (WYSIWYG).

If you already have web space, or can acquire it, then you can write e-learning to it. The learning is hosted on a server that learners access online to undertake the learning. But you may want to limit who can access it, via the security of user names and passwords. You may want to offer a portal, or point of entry to the learning, welcoming learners, giving key information, and offering choices; you may want to restrict who can see and/or access each course. You may want to include complicated simulations or animations, audio or video, or secure assessment. You may want to generate reports on learner progress, especially with assessments. And you may want to link your e-learning to other platforms or systems within your organization. You can build all this from scratch on any website, but doing so can be technically complex, expensive and time-consuming. Hence, there are ready-designed e-learning technologies that anticipate your needs. The sections that follow explain them in more detail.

VIRTUAL LEARNING ENVIRONMENTS

Virtual learning environments (VLEs) represent the most commonly discussed, and generally the biggest and most expensive, e-learning software. You do not actually need a virtual learning environment to implement e-learning, so why is there an international industry in providing 'enterprise solutions' based on them, and why does nearly every university and college have one (or more)? The answer is that these learning platforms, as they are sometimes called, can do all the things described in the previous paragraph. VLEs often also include further software that we will discuss under the headings that follow.

Sometimes VLEs go by other names, such as 'managed learning environments', but some other terms that are used for them actually have more specific meanings. A VLE can include a learner management system, a learning content management system and a virtual classroom, plus other, ancillary functions (see Figure 4.1).

A *learner management system* (LMS) is a means of manipulating information about learners. By building a database of learners, you can track their

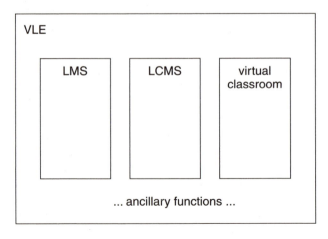

Figure 4.1 Structure of a VLE

progress as they go through courses, and can generate reports classified in many ways, such as by learning route, occupation, location, gender, age profile, etc. The bigger the organization, the more useful this information can be. One drawback to an LMS is that its benefits really depend on economies of scale (so it is of limited value to a small business or any relatively small learning community). Another is that the information in its reports tends to comprise metrics about 'housekeeping' rather than performance improvement. It can tell you a lot about how well it works within its own parameters, but not so much about how it adds value to your organization.

A *learning content management system* (LCMS) is a means of organizing the learning – a repository for storing, retrieving and launching courses or their components. An LCMS can generate reports too, such as reports on the uptake of courses, or on success rates. But the real benefits are in managing the learning content, and so an LCMS should be used in tandem with an authoring tool (see below); indeed, many include an authoring tool. This combination enables the user to write and store courses and their building blocks, reusable learning objects (see below). The main drawback of an LCMS is its focus on 'content' rather than learning experiences; it is really just a slightly specialized version of a generic software application, the content management system, used in various information processing contexts.

A *virtual classroom* is a means of staging learning events for participants in different locations. The virtual classroom is a development from the technology for video conferencing and online meetings, to enable online lectures, seminars, tutorials and discussion workshops – all kinds of live e-learning. It works by using webcams and screens for visual contact, and microphones and speakers or headsets for audio contact. Shared screen space takes the place of the chalkboard or flipchart or slide projector, and shared access to documents is enabled. The drawbacks to the virtual classroom are that not enough thought has gone into the specific needs of learning events rather than generic virtual meetings, and the limited range of contact means that it is always a poor substitute for real face-to-face events. However, if properly used, this technology can be very powerful.

The virtual classroom is a good example of technology for a *synchronous* e-learning experience, one where learners 'get together' (in their various locations) at the same times, as distinct from an *asynchronous* e-learning experience, where learners can undertake the same e-learning at different times and at their own pace. The virtual classroom is the ideal software application for model 4, live e-learning.

In the past couple of years there has been much speculation about *personal VLEs*. The idea of these is that individuals should be able to organize their own personal learning space online, linking to all the content, tools and resources that are useful to them, including their lifelong learning record and their e-portfolio and/or blog, if they have them. Advocates of personal VLEs contend that they will offer not just greater personalization and flexibility for each individual, but more economical and more effective learning resources for organizations. Nobody is very clear about how we get there from the starting point of current, proprietary VLEs, but it seems likely that this development will emerge from commoditization of VLE software, more (and more reliable) open-source software, and the commercial demise of current VLE vendors. This looks problematical, given the scale of the VLE sector and the investment in VLEs by corporate and academic users alike, yet it does seem a likely trend.

AUTHORING TOOLS

If you are familiar with a computer programming language, you can use it to create web pages and anything on them. Authoring tools enable anyone who does not have programming skills to do the same.

Typically, they include options to enable you to create fairly quickly the sort of features you will want over and over again, such as blocks of text, images, document attachments, links to other sites, and perhaps audio or video or animations. They may include templates for simple features such as 'conceal-and-reveal', where the learner is invited to reflect on a statement and then can click on the concealed part to reveal some feedback. This is an example of interactivity to make the learner more active in the learning process and to provide formative assessment.

Authoring tools usually also include simple capabilities to provide both formative and summative assessment by creating multiple-choice questions or quizzes. Learning professionals usually find the scope of these very limited and look for more sophisticated options (see the next section on e-assessment).

Most authoring tools will enable you to author content that is compliant with various standards such as those cited in the e-learning standards section above, and some will name other proprietary systems with which they ensure specific compatibility. The ability to create reusable learning objects should ensure compatibility with most learning content management systems. The benefit of this is that you can build courses comprising common objects and only need to update one object to ensure that its application in many courses is automatically updated.

Learning objects take the concept of modularization of learning to its logical extreme. Some people have, almost jokingly, called it 'granularization' or 'disaggregation' or 'chunking'. Each object is the smallest possible stand-alone element of learning, such as a single fact or formula, the statement of a concept, or their expressions in an image or a sound clip. These objects can then be combined – used and reused – as required.

Since the concept of reusable learning objects was first mooted, it has been claimed that it will save time for developers, avoid repetitive work ('reinventing the wheel') and equip organizations with banks of objects that can be assembled into new courses. The reality has – so far, at least – failed to live up to this expectation, as developers often prefer to build anew, and it is increasingly easy and inexpensive to do so.

E-ASSESSMENT

Automated assessment is a controversial subject. Whenever you hear a discussion of the subject, it seems that some people, especially laypeople, think that problems of plagiarism and impersonation arise from the internet, when the reality is that the power of the internet has brought to the fore issues that should always have been of concern.

E-assessment has been proven to work very well where the form of assessment is relatively simple: true/false answers, multiple-choice questions, 'hotspot' questions (where the learner has to click on the right part of a diagram or map) and the like. When the learner has to write in an answer, things get more difficult, as the assessment author has to anticipate all possible misspellings and other near-correct answers that should be scored as correct. Beyond this, perhaps the ultimate goal of e-assessment is consistently accurate marking of free-text answers such as essay submissions. There are programs that can score large amounts of writing for style, but marking it for content is much tougher because the input requirements of one-word write-in answers are multiplied many times. It can be done, but so far the technology does not help the input to be any less laborious. Until this problem is overcome, manual assessment will continue to hold an advantage here.

Nevertheless, e-assessment provides a fast, accurate and consistent means of scoring relatively simple tests, and there are plenty of options available for the buyer that are of no greater complexity than the VLE and authoring systems they complement. Relatively simple e-assessment tools are often built into VLEs and authoring tools, but there are also specialist vendors, such as QMark, concentrating in this field alone and offering more elaborate assessment opportunities.

One more specialized area is that of *e-portfolios*, which are a development of evidence-based assessment systems and are common in vocational learning schemes such as for professional qualifications. The old paper-based versions were often, deservedly, criticized for generating huge amounts of paper disproportionate to what was being measured. The electronic versions therefore represent a significant step forward, with all the records being stored online.

SPECIALIST SOFTWARE

Some of the more specialized content that can populate a VLE is provided by vendors that specialize in a particular kind of software. It includes:

- *Simulations*, sometimes shortened to Sims, which can be as simple as animated graphs or diagrams that change as you adjust the variables, or more complex representations of real-life activities such as the operation of machinery or even virtual surgery – or, as a further abstraction, representations of activities in an imaginary world.

- *Games*, which provide a learning experience as players progress through game activities. These can range from simple games that are little more than self-assessment activities, to highly complex contests involving many players and different levels of strategy and tactics. For those who like playing games (most people?), they inject an element of fun.

- *Revision tools*, raging from relatively simple study guides to animated multi-media mind-maps.

- *Virtual characters*, or animated avatars, to guide and help the learner as a live tutor would.

- *Three-dimensional (3D) panoramic imaging*, which can be used to guide the learner around facilities or equipment, buildings or machinery, with dynamic and interactive features to assist learning.

This is not an exhaustive list. There are many examples of specialist software than can enhance the learning experience, and most are designed to be easy to use, and to integrate with VLEs.

WIKIS, BLOGS, FORUMS AND PODCASTS

There is a growing recognition, in the application of ICT to learning, that learning is less about *information* and more about *communication*. This has led to a number of developments that collectively help characterize 'e-learning 2.0' (see Chapter 1), or the work-oriented learning applications of social networking. From a technological viewpoint these are tools that can be used outside a virtual learning environment; from a marketing viewpoint they are helping raise awareness of e-learning, and perhaps improving its reputation among those who have been sceptical about VLEs.

Wikis are websites where users can share the development of content and discuss their progress. The best-known wiki collaboration is the worldwide, multi-language encyclopedia Wikipedia, which has 1,000 administrators and includes a core group of 4,000 people making over 100 edits per month (2007 figures). The same principle is used to develop e-learning content, including user-generated content, and to provide a forum for learners to share contributions. The latter works especially well in blended learning – the second model in our typology of e-learning – where learners may want to exchange information after a face-to-face session.

Blogs – a contraction from 'web-logs' – are like online diaries, or logs, where the 'blogger' regularly writes and publishes ('posts') his or her ideas and opinions. For e-learning, these can be useful for tutors providing ongoing information for learners, and there is a degree of interactivity, as readers can post comments or questions to the blogger, which can lead to wider discussion. And, of course, any learner can set up their own blog, which can lead to extensive networking of blogs with related themes. There are several versions of blogging software available, free to set up, publish and update – and easy enough for anyone to use. As evidence, and with no false modesty, I offer the example of my own blog, started in 2007: http://learnforeverblog.blogspot.com.

Discussion forums seem like the least fashionable of the 'new' participative tools, perhaps because it is most apparent that they are not in fact new. In a discussion forum, any user can write and publish (again, 'post') a new topic for discussion, and responses are shown within a discussion 'thread'. Thus, learners may simply read discussion threads posted by others, or may choose to contribute to existing discussions, or may initiate new ones themselves if they wish to become more active. Discussion forums are very common on many websites, quite apart from their use for learning, but have a mixed reputation because some forums are underused, and when this is the case the application looks unimpressive. However, a well-used and well-moderated forum (moderators may prompt and guide discussions, merge related discussions, and move or delete inappropriate contributions) can be an invaluable learning aid. An alternative, less descriptive, term for a discussion forum is a bulletin board; this harks back to when the use of the forum was little understood and it was expected to be used for the posting of notices, as more of an information than a communication tool.

Podcasts are audio or video clips that may be downloaded to a user's handheld device such as an iPod, whence the name (although this derivation is sometimes disputed). They may also, of course, be viewed or listened to on a desktop or laptop PC. Podcasting can be seen as a much more targeted variant of traditional broadcasting.

OTHER USEFUL CONCEPTS

Instant messaging is a favourite of the young digital natives, for whom e-mail can be just not fast enough. It works like an enhanced version of texting by mobile phone except that it is done using any PC or handheld, it shows the message (conversation) history, it can accommodate attached files and hyperlinks, and it can be used for group discussions, not just one-to-one messages. An e-learning group comfortable with instant messaging can run it alongside another shared resource, such as a wiki, but such use is eclipsed by a good virtual classroom, which should include a similar facility.

RSS feeds are an increasingly common feature of busy websites where users want to be alerted to new information as it is published, and busy e-learning sites should be no different. If a website is being updated several times a day, as will especially be the case with participative applications such as wikis and forums, and users are visiting the site frequently, then RSS feeds can ensure that learners are directed to the most up-to-date content. RSS is used as an abbreviation for several similar phrases, but is generally understood to stand for Really Simple Syndication.

Rapid content development is a term for tools that enable e-learning material to be published more quickly, and the accompanying concept that less-structured content gives learners greater control over how they learn. The term also describes a development process whereby, rather than the content going through various iterations of e-learning until finally a version is arrived at that is fully approved for use, an imperfect but usable version is made available as soon as possible, and any further improvements are made after learning from its actual use. Most authoring tools describe themselves as suitable for rapid content development, which rather dilutes the concept.

Bandwidth limitations inhibit the adoption of anything that requires the user to download large files such as audio and video. It is still important for some organizations to take account of the needs of learners using dial-up connections or constrained by busy corporate networks, but the increasingly widespread uptake of more and more powerful broadband connections means this is much less of a problem, and will be even less so in the future.

M-learning is an abbreviation for mobile learning. You might well ask why we need another term for what is really just the use of a different digital technology device to undertake e-learning. We don't, of course, but, as we have already observed, this is an industry that spawns unnecessary jargon. Some commentators, including Martyn Sloman, argue that mobile learning will always have limited application because the screens of handheld devices are too small to show enough content or enough detail. Others, like Allison Rossett, contend that handhelds are ideal for employees on the move, to view product updates, watch demos and keep in contact with colleagues who want to discuss these developments. Allison argues that there will be more e-learning like this in the future, and I suspect she is right.

At a conference in London in 2001, I met a man who claimed to have invented something called _T-learning_. He told me it stood for television-based learning and that it would revolutionize the way people learned, especially in the home. Seven years later there has been no discernible progress with this idea, but yet another piece of new jargon was created instantly, disseminated at that conference and remained in circulation afterwards. There is a kernel of usefulness in this idea, which we will return to before the end of this book.

KISS is not a technology but a philosophy. It stands for 'Keep It Simple, Stupid'. Sometimes vendors (and others) lose sight of it, but it is a useful check to make on anything that seems to be getting over-complicated, and a good concept to quote when trying to cut through techie jargon. As Freeman Dyson said, 'The technologies which have had the most profound effects on human life are usually simple.'

Further information about all of the technologies discussed in this section can be found online, but see the glossary at the end of this book for a short summary of each term.

E-LEARNING SUPPLIERS: IDENTIFYING, CLASSIFYING, SELECTING AND MANAGING THEM

Earlier in this chapter, we identified six different types of e-learning suppliers:

- consultants;
- writers/developers;
- generic courseware vendors;
- learning platform, or VLE, providers;
- authoring tools providers;
- providers of specialist software.

Your strategic relationship with your supplier(s) is critical to the success of your e-learning, so it is important that you understand what the supplier can and cannot contribute. Decide for yourself what your supplier's core competence is, avoid asking them to move too far away from it, and resist any attempts by them to expand beyond it.

Suppliers can be sourced in a number of ways, from web searches to the visiting of exhibitions, or they can find you through their sales and marketing activities. The best way is often by recommendation from another satisfied client. If you find your supplier by another route, you should always seek testimonials from clients for whom the supplier has undertaken work similar to what you need.

There is plenty of guidance available on selecting suppliers. For example, Don Morrison offers a 10-step procedure in *E-learning Strategies* (see Chapter 7 of this book). There is less help on how to manage them effectively. Perhaps the best advice is to treat them rather like employees: establish a clear contract, think of them as partners, communicate as much as possible and be clear about where they fit in the big picture. The key difference from an employer–employee relationship (at least a permanent one) is that your supplier relationship is much more likely to be time bound, to be short term. Accordingly, you need to plan for when the relationship will end, be open with the supplier about this from the outset, and follow your timescale, reviewing as necessary.

Clients often feel vulnerable when dealing with e-learning suppliers because the suppliers appear to know so much more about e-learning that they have the scope to take advantage of, and even defraud, their clients in various ways. This is not strictly true, but suppliers do often have a much better understanding of the technological aspects. Further information about how to combat this is widely available, such as Kevin Kruse's discussion of what he calls 'tricks, traps and other e-learning vendor shenanigans' on the E-learning Guru website (the specific reference is given in Chapter 7). Kruse cites six areas to be especially careful about: who owns the source code, who owns the content, whether expenses are extra, what updates will cost, whether you are being constrained by the use of proprietary software and whether the vendor is subcontracting work to freelances. This advice is helpful, and we certainly need to be wary of unscrupulous suppliers, but in general we need to approach supplier relationships in a more positive way.

Although this book contains many criticisms of supplier behaviour in the e-learning marketplace, this should not be taken to imply that the market is full of crooks, or that dishonesty is commonplace. Rather, there has been a herd effect: many vendors' behaviour has been influenced by others, and perhaps also by the defensive behaviour of clients.

Good supplier relationships can be invaluable in implementing e-learning.

TWENTY THINGS TO BE WARY OF WITH VENDORS

The following list does not, of course, apply to every vendor, but summarizes common bad practice by vendors – bad practice that learning and development professionals need to recognize and approach with caution.

1. E-learning vendors have encouraged the view that e-learning is completely different from learning; it's not.

2. Vendors' definitions of e-learning are often misleading because they are often devised to lend disproportionate importance to their own offers.

3. Vendors frequently use technological jargon to mystify e-learning, when they should be trying to make it more accessible.

4. Vendors rarely know much about learning, yet often profess to be experts in e-learning; they're not.

5. Vendors often claim to offer complete e-learning solutions, when in fact they usually offer expertise only in one part.

6. Vendors tend to exaggerate the importance of their products and services.

7. Vendors overemphasize the importance of (their) technology, when in fact it is just one of three component parts of e-learning.

8. Vendors have a simplistic notion of what is involved in learning, which leads them to offer technology of limited value and to miss opportunities for what technology could achieve.

9. Vendors' simplistic understanding of learning also leads to poor e-learning implementations.

10. 'E-learning 2.0' is mystifying jargon deployed by vendors to cover up their past failures while offering the same products as before.

11. The benefits vendors claim for e-learning serve more to make the vendor's business case than to identify real benefits for their clients. (For example, 'scalability' helps vendors target larger clients, but is meaningless for small to medium-sized clients.)

12. Vendors typically just sell their own, standard, products, rather than helping identify clients' problems and finding solutions for them.

13. Vendors often propose unique approaches to the development and implementation of e-learning, when learning and development professionals already have planning models that will work just as well for e-learning.

14. Vendors are rarely interested in learning strategy development, just in selling their own products.

15. Vendors tend to have a better understanding of technology issues than their clients have, but they do not always share it in an open and honest way.

16. Vendors overemphasize the importance of e-learning technology standards and specifications.

17. Vendors will sometimes give clients assurances of standards compliance when in fact they are being economical with the truth and their 'compliance' does not address the client's needs.

18. Vendors may seek to infringe on clients' intellectual property rights.

19. Vendors sometimes offer misleading price information, excluding items such as updates or expenses, which can make up a high proportion of clients' real costs.

20. Vendors will sometimes covertly subcontract work to freelances, exposing clients to a greater degree of risk than is made clear.

Again, I must stress that, despite the prevalence of so much bad practice, good vendors, and good vendor relationships, are invaluable to the implementation of successful e-learning. E-learning vendors, as well as learning and development professionals, would do well to heed the lessons of these 20 points.

WORKING TO A BUDGET

Whatever your budget, you will need to be careful about what you spend. Here are some guidelines on the relative prices you may be charged, and how you can manage these costs. Prices will vary from country to country, and fluctuate with economic conditions, but for ease of conversion I offer rough prices in US dollars.

The biggest investment of all in e-learning is likely to be the learning platform (unless you pay for the development of lots of video or complex simulation or other high-design content). A proprietary VLE will usually cost tens of thousands of US dollars for a corporate licence. Even an entry-level commitment, perhaps a pilot scheme, is still likely to run to five figures. Related costs, such as hosting on a server, and software support and maintenance, are likely to be extra. As this is a capital investment, and will be utilized and depreciated over time, it is reasonable to require the vendor to offer a payment plan and not expect payment in full upfront, or even in the first year. Open-source VLEs are an alternative that will be free of any licence fees but will still require hosting and technical support, although the cost of the support at least should depend on how much you actually use. Links to some examples of open-source VLEs are given in Chapter 7.

Authoring tools vary in price but can usually be purchased for a few hundred dollars, or no more than $2,000. Of course, if you purchase a learning platform it is likely to include authoring capability already, so this cost is avoidable unless you want enhanced capability that your VLE cannot offer.

It is harder to estimate prices for more specialized software (although open-source alternatives will always be free). Some of these were once priced highly and unrealistically by vendors who thought their offerings were world-beaters. A sense of realism has set in since the dotcom bubble burst, but it is still possible to pay tens of thousands of dollars to develop bespoke solutions.

Video production has always been seen as a specialized (and expensive) field, but with a basic webcam priced from about $30, including software, you can record simple video clips of satisfactory quality and load them to your learning platform or website. Websites like YouTube have shown how easy it is, and now that anyone can direct their own movie, there is no reason why learning and development professionals should not get in on the act. Such clips could include 'talking heads' – for example, a senior manager making a short welcoming statement filmed head and shoulders only from a single fixed camera position, or slightly more ambitious views of corporate buildings or plant. Short lectures or presentations can be recorded in the same way (longer ones need more than one camera angle and some editing, so professional help would be better), as can interviews or other relatively limited situations. The same applies to audio recordings, only more so: unless you have very ambitious sound recording needs, you can do it cheaply, and probably better, yourself. Never underestimate the power of a local accent!

Animation has also traditionally been seen as specialized and expensive, but some tools require very little training for users to create their own simple animations. The most popular software, from Adobe, sells for less than $500 in the United States (a bit more elsewhere), and training to use it can be even cheaper.

In general, it pays to shop around. For almost any element of e-learning there is a 'deluxe' version and an 'economy' version (and everything in between). You don't always get what you pay for, so you need to judge value for yourself.

Illustrative project

Considering what technologies to use was tricky. I didn't know much about them, or even what was possible, but I knew what we wanted to achieve, so that was my guide.

I arranged to meet several e-learning providers to find out more. From our initial conversations they all seemed to offer similar things, but when they came in and demonstrated their products, I realized there was a huge variety of offers. I started to look for specialization, because I wanted to work with people who were experts at what they did, but stuck to that and let us be experts in our business.

I decided we didn't need to buy one of the expensive systems we were offered, but to retain consultants who could advise on how to build the e-learning, choose an authoring tool, help us with the initial design, then back off. We published an invitation to tender and met with several firms before selecting consultants we felt we could work with. The winning tender proposed creating our own dedicated website for learning, secured with user names and passwords, and built on an open-source platform with its own authoring tool.

SUMMARY OF KEY POINTS

1. There is too much technological jargon associated with e-learning, and too many technology vendors use it to obfuscate e-learning.

2. The e-learning industry, in so far as such a thing exists, is very fragmented.

3. There are six categories of e-learning vendor: consultants; authors or developers; generic courseware vendors; virtual learning environment (VLE) providers; authoring tool providers; and providers of specialist software. Most vendors have core competence in just one of these categories.

4. The question of e-learning standards is a hot topic in e-learning but is largely irrelevant for most of us. We should understand that SCORM (Sharable Content Object Reference Model) is a collection of standards and specifications to enable interoperability, accessibility and reusability of web-based learning content, but we should not be enslaved by it.

5. A virtual learning environment is an enabling system for e-learning, which can be expensive but can be invaluable, especially for large organizations that need scalable solutions. A VLE may include a learner management system (LMS), a learning content management system (LCMS) and a virtual classroom.

6. Authoring tools may be used by non-techies to create their own e-learning, often relatively quickly and easily, as in rapid content development, either independently or within a virtual learning environment.

7. There is a variety of additional specialist software available, notably e-assessment software, that may also be used independently or within a VLE.

8. Some of the more recently adopted software options, such as wikis, blogs, discussion forums and podcasts, increase the potential for

learner participation, and for more interactive, and therefore more effective, e-learning.

9.   Supplier relationships need to be managed in a positive way to make the most of them, and to add the maximum value.

5

E-learning strategy: learning design issues

In this chapter we consider the strategic importance of e-learning design, includ-
ing its relationship to other strategic considerations. We draw from broader
design rules and guidelines, establish our own five general principles for effective
e-learning design, plus two underlying principles, and we apply them to design
approaches for each model of e-learning. Finally, we observe that the theory of e-
learning design is still evolving.

STRATEGIC DESIGN

If the first aspect of e-learning strategy is strategy development and the
second aspect is management of suppliers and resources, then the third
aspect of e-learning strategy is e-learning design.

In Chapter 1 we looked at the three components of e-learning: technology, content and learning design. Also, we distinguished five models of
e-learning. In this chapter we will move on to consider how to design the
learning for each model. This is a strategic decision, and should no more
be left to chance than any other aspect of your e-learning strategy.

Before we do that, let's recap. We can distinguish the 'stuff' of learning
– the subject content and the enabling technology – from the 'stir' – the
way that the learning is shaped and delivered to the learner, and the sort
of learning experience that is designed. We can then identify three com-

plementary components of e-learning: the technology, the content and the design. The design is what brings together the technology and the content, as well as adding something of its own, and this is now our focus.

Without strategic design, the learning is constructed in a random way, and we can have no confidence that learners will achieve their goals. Design is a strategic issue because your organization needs a shared sense of how your e-learning is deployed, how it works and what sort of 'look' and 'feel' it has. Otherwise, you will just be making a series of tactical e-learning interventions, some of which may work while others won't, but which, taken together, will not have a collective coherence.

Design can sometimes be underestimated as being just a routine technical exercise about how to place items on the page or screen, and adjust colours and styles. In this view it has no real impact on the substance of learning. But strategic design is much more important than that: it is about the emotional impact of the learning, about how learners experience it. In a nutshell, well-designed e-learning works; poorly designed e-learning doesn't. Therefore, we need to take a strategic approach to e-learning design.

When we look at design, we are starting to examine the specifics of e-learning, starting to apply our strategic thinking to a practical application. This demonstrates that strategy is not just lofty idealizing or empty theory. It means we are linking theory with practice, and not developing a strategy for the business without relating it to the fundamentals of what e-learning is intrinsically about. You can have the most business-focused strategy in the world, but if at its core there is bland or ineffective e-learning – or worse, e-learning that turns off learners – then your strategy will fail. Therefore, e-learning design is a vital strategic issue.

WHY DESIGN MATTERS

As Paola Antonelli of the Museum of Modern Art in New York says, 'good design is a Renaissance attitude that combines technology, cognitive science, human need and beauty to produce something'. It is a lofty ideal, but also quite down-to-earth. Design is about bringing things together, and this is always important, but perhaps never more so than when there are disparate elements to reconcile, such as technology and content in learning. The Antonelli quotation makes it sound complicated, but design is about communicating clearly, using whatever tools and whatever media are to hand – and clarity demands simplicity.

When learning and development is just a question of preparing for face-to-face learning events, or writing for a text-dominated publication, as in distance learning, then design is less important. But e-learning is a visual medium, as much about images (including moving images) as about the written word. And it is about, or should be about, an enormous range of different inputs, including written text, the spoken word, numbers, tables, charts, graphs, diagrams, drawings, photographs, photo-stories, videos, animation, music, background noise, sound effects, plus countless opportunities for intervention by learners themselves. Learning design – the orchestration of these elements – thus becomes critical.

When Antonelli uses the term 'Renaissance', I believe she intends it in the sense of the multidisciplinary approach typified in figures of the Renaissance period of history such as Leonardo da Vinci, whose knowledge and skill extended across a broad spectrum of science and arts. Samantha Chapnick and Jimm Meloy mean it in a different sense in the title of their book *Renaissance eLearning: Creating dramatic and unconventional learning experiences*, where it refers to the word's literal meaning of a *rebirth* of e-learning, embracing creativity and imaginative design derived from other fields and applied to the relatively new field of e-learning.

Chapnick and Meloy suggest a number of 'universal design principles' that they contend are accepted by designers in many disciplines. These seem to represent good general guidance for e-learning designers:

- The *aesthetic usability principle*, which basically means making it look as good as possible on the grounds that this will appeal more to users. For e-learners, this means ensuring a degree of comfort with the learning, that unattractive content does not jar and that it appeals on a subconscious level.

- *Consistency*, which means that similar parts are expressed in similar ways. For e-learning, this means that navigation is eased by signposting and simple rules, and colour schemes and graphical layouts follow a logical pattern.

- The *Pareto principle*, also known as the 80–20 rule, meaning that 80 per cent of the functionality will be used by just 20 per cent of users, and vice versa. In e-learning, this suggests that many features could be wasted, but also that the learning will need to be effective even if learners use just 20 per cent of the features.

- Using *proximity*, a concept that comes from Gestalt psychology and suggests that things positioned close together are perceived as closely related. For e-learning, this means that layout and the alignment of objects help learners make mental connections.

- The *LATCH principle* for ordering information, where LATCH stands for Location, Alphabet, Time, Category and Hierarchy. In e-learning, these provide guidance on appropriate sequences for presenting information to ensure maximum potential for mental retention and recollection.

We can also learn from the general principles of web design, with its classification of web pages as either *static* (fixed, unchanging pages) or *dynamic* (those that change according to user input). General web design principles also address the sequential processes of planning, modelling and execution of web pages, and are concerned about their visibility (searchability, how easy they are to find, etc), usability (navigation and related issues) and appearance (colours and graphics), as well as their contents. This is not just about aesthetics but about how the user interacts with the website, which has useful (albeit incomplete) parallels with learners' experiences in e-learning.

All this amounts to good advice, and suggests that further study of overall design principles could yield further insights for developing e-learning. Design is a discipline that learning and development professionals need to take seriously, not least because learning design involves much more than design in general. Learning design is about what makes learning work. Building on that, we shall move on to establish our own general design principles for e-learning.

DESIGN FOR THE LEARNER

Implicit in all of this, and following our philosophy of leaner-centred learning, is the underlying principle that we are designing for the learner. This may seem glaringly obvious, but it is surprising how much e-learning seems to have been designed for other reasons, such as to allow developers to try out different tools and techniques, or to satisfy the whims of managers or trainers who will not actually be experiencing the learning.

Like all other aspects of e-learning strategy, learning design needs to be approached from the learner's perspective. People often tell me you need to be very motivated to undertake e-learning. This is true; indeed, you need to be motivated to undertake any sort of learning. If you are not motivated, you won't learn. End of story. E-learning has the advantage that it brings this issue to the surface; it doesn't have the problem of classroom 'presenteeism' (the corollary of absenteeism), where learners show up but doze off (sometimes literally) and do not actually learn anything. With e-learning, when someone isn't learning, they are quickly spotted.

However, we do need to bear in mind, when designing e-learning, that often there is no tutor present, or anyone else to support the learners, other than themselves. This has important implications. When we design e-learning, we need to think like a learner.

Those of us who were relatively successful at school, went on to higher education, obtained a degree and perhaps postgraduate qualifications, have undertaken vocational training, pursue continuous professional development, branch out into research and educational interests of our own, support our children's schooling, enjoy learning for its own sake, and indeed in some cases make our living from learning and development, need a reality check: we need constantly to remind ourselves that many people do not have such a happy relationship with learning. This is a classic teacher–learner dilemma.

Unless we make learning interesting, stimulating, amusing, entertaining, intriguing, engaging and exciting, we will lose many learners. We need to retain their attention and make them want to move on to the next bit.

Unless we provide a direct route to essential learning, many learners will not follow it. Unlike us, they will not pursue interesting side-tracks, because they won't see the point; they won't be motivated to do so.

Yet this doesn't mean e-learning needs to be *too* directive, as down that route lies stultifying, dull learning, and perhaps therefore no learning at all. We need to find a middle road where the directions are clear but there is scope for the imagination of the willing learner.

DESIGN FOR PURPOSE

In the introduction to this book I put forward two enduring truths about learning: first, that it is about the learner; and second, that it is about a purpose. Our second underlying principle is that, just as design needs to be for the learner, it also needs to be for a clear purpose.

E-learning, like all learning, needs to have clear aims and objectives for the learners, and everything within the e-learning, including readings, resources, activities and assessments (more on these later), needs to be designed to meet these aims and objectives. More than that, the e-learning needs to have a purpose in terms of what it seeks to achieve for the organization, not just for the individual learners.

The wider goals of e-learning may be expressed in a number of ways, although ultimately these should be about business results. (There is further guidance on this in the next chapter.) Learning and development professionals have always sought to dissect the essential activities of a business in ways that will help the design of learning interventions, such as through job analysis, task analysis, skills analysis and, more recently, functional analysis.

There is a powerful focus in many organizations on competence. Skills analyses yield behavioural competences, which define the skills or behaviours needed to perform a task or fulfil a job role. Alternatively, functional analyses yield functional competences, which define the outputs expected from individual job roles, work groups, departments, divisions or business units, and entire organizations. Thus, e-learning designed to address this kind of functionality can provide a map and compass for the development of an entire organization.

Some organizations have moved beyond a focus on competence to concentrate instead on the strengths and talents of their workforce. Talent management is often seen as matching these strengths and talents to overall business objectives. Essentially, this is another model for tying learning, including e-learning, activities to broader strategies.

When designing e-learning, we need to keep in mind the goals of the organization, and a sense of what we are trying to achieve. This helps maintain consistency, it provides a focus for the learner and it maintains a strategic perspective.

These two underlying principles, of design for the learner and design for purpose, lead us to the five general principles that follow.

THE FIVE GENERAL PRINCIPLES

There are five essential considerations for effective e-learning design, common to all the e-learning models. These are general rules governing the development, organization and presentation of e-learning, and I call them our five general principles (Figure 5.1):

1. It should be a managed programme.

2. It should be an effective learning experience.

3. It should be a learning process, not just 'e-reading'.

4. It should use technology to enhance learning.

5. It should take advantage of the strengths of the web.

Let's look at each of these principles in turn.

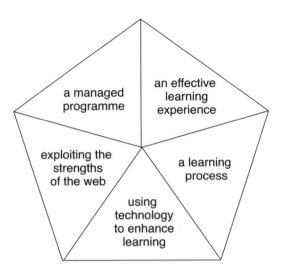

Figure 5.1 Design principles

1. A managed programme

The first principle, that the programme should be managed, is a general rule for all learning programmes, not just e-learning. Any old course of education can achieve outcomes for the learner, but if you want to be able to transfer learning to the workplace and achieve measurable business outcomes (see the next chapter), then you need a disciplined framework. This should include a system of quality assurance, a plan for evaluation and a focus on results (again, see the next chapter). As we discussed in Chapter 3, you need both to manage the integral programme processes – ensuring learner completions, compliance with deadlines, achievement of outcomes, system efficiencies and so on – and to ensure the external validity of the course, managing its transfer and application, and its impact on real business outcomes. Your design must allow learners to achieve all their outcomes, and the business to achieve all of its results.

Without a managed programme, there is chaos; with a managed programme, everything else starts to fall into place. Vendors of learner management systems (see the previous chapter) often exploit this generic issue to make claims for their products, but the truth is not that you necessarily need to adopt an LMS, but that you need to be organized.

A managed e-learning programme includes a project plan in which the roles of all key personnel are clearly defined. It includes defined outcomes such as shared aims and specific learner objectives. It includes a system of quality assurance. It includes a system of evaluation. It fits clearly into the wider scope of the learning and development function, and enjoys a recognized place in the organization. It is the foundation, and provides a secure context, for all other design principles.

Having a managed e-learning programme is the first essential principle for effective e-learning design.

2. An effective learning experience

Designing a course is not the same thing as designing a learning experience. Experiential learning means people learning through what they do and what they discover for themselves. You can plan how these acts and discoveries will happen, and thus direct learning towards planned outcomes, but it needs to be something the learners undertake for themselves. In other words, it needs to be learner centred.

In learning for work, courses need to be more than courses in the academic world: because they aim to do something meaningful for the organization as well as the individual, they need to have high relevance and obvious impact in the workplace. These courses, including online courses, need to be learning experiences. Like traditional coaching, e-coaching needs to be a learning experience. Online learning resources need to offer opportunities for not just for self-study but for learning experiences. Virtual classroom events, to be successful, need to be successful learning experiences. Every kind of online learning needs to be an experience.

It needs to offer an active, not a passive, learning experience, which means learners need to become engaged, think through issues and solve problems. There needs to be plenty of scope for interactivity: interactivity with the technology, interactivity among learners, and interactivity with people in support roles, including managers, mentors and tutors. You need to find ways to engage different parts of the brain. You need to make sure, wherever possible, that the learning experience is both memorable and fun. And you need to take account of different learning style preferences (see Chapter 2).

Max Frisch described technology as 'the knack of so arranging the world that we don't have to experience it'. However apt this may be in other fields, it cannot be so in e-learning if the learning is to succeed.

3. A learning process, not just 'e-reading'

You need to focus more on the learning process than the content. This means creating a learning structure whereby the learner has a navigational guide through the learning. There should be a clear route for the learner to follow, with readings, assessments, and other resources and activities offered as branches from the main route, not as part of the main route itself. This is evidently true of live e-learning, when you would not expect someone to read during the lesson, but is also true of online or blended courses, where the readings should be slightly to one side and not lead people away from the path they are following.

To persist with readings as an example, you should never expect learners to accept screeds of reading material in the main body of the course or programme. Rather, you should place readings as attachments (PDFs, Word documents, or similar), offer links to readings already available on the web and offer reading lists for offline books, journals, etc. The worst kind of e-learning consists of screen after screen of content to read. This is 'e-reading' and should be avoided at all costs.

Too many e-learning designers, paying homage to the king of content, focus more on getting the content right – and of course it needs to be accurate and comprehensive – when instead they should be focusing more on how people will learn. That is what effective design is about.

Which is not to say reading is not an important part of e-learning; of course it is, and people should be encouraged to read. But they need to choose how and when they read, on-screen or printed off to paper, and we need to recognize that large volumes of reading material are off-putting and, moreover, can confuse key messages. As screen sizes get bigger, screen resolution improves and people get more used to reading from a screen, the problem of e-reading becomes less marked, but the issues of variety and interactivity remain, and we will increasingly need to anticipate the needs of learners using small screens on handhelds, which are certainly not conducive to extensive reading.

One of the most common mistakes made by newcomers to offering learning is to think of learning simply in terms of the classic transmitter–receiver (Tx–Rx) communication model (Figure 5.2).

In this model, information, such as from a speaker or writer, is transferred to a listener or reader (which is what is happening as you read these lines). In e-learning, this means information being communicated by the trainer to the learner. In crude terms, this kind of communication takes place all the time in our lives and work, including e-learning, but it is also an oversimplification of the learning process, and a misleading one at that.

The next extension of this model introduces a vital new element of complexity, the feedback loop (Figure 5.3).

Tx   Rx

Figure 5.2 Transmitter–receiver model

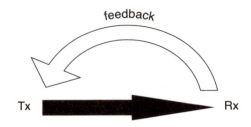

Figure 5.3 Feedback loop

The feedback loop shows how the receiver acknowledges receipt of information and gives further guidance to the transmitter. This is vital for effective communication to take place, as without the feedback loop the transmitter is blindly sending out information without any indication of whether any of it is actually communicated. In e-learning, we have to have a feedback loop so that learners can let trainers know whether they understand the information, and what they make of it; this in turn enables the trainer to adjust the information to help the learner learn better or learn more.

But learning is more complex still. For effective learning we need to escape the model of the trainer as the fount of all knowledge and the learner as the empty vessel to be filled. In fact, learners have much to contribute themselves, and e-learning tools such as blogs, wikis and discussion forums take advantage of this. Learners can tell trainers, and other learners, about their experiences in the workplace, and relevant past experiences. Learners can enrich the learning experience by sharing their knowledge and expertise. The effective trainer is really more of a facilitator of learning, because he or she recognizes that his or her role is to draw and build upon the experiences of everyone involved in the process.

Thus, an important principle of effective learning design is to see learning as an all-inclusive process in which everyone contributes, rather than simply the output of teaching or training, and to plan on that basis.

4. Using technology to enhance learning

It seems obvious to say that effective design should involve using technology to enable learning and to enhance the learning experience, yet this fundamental point is often overlooked. Sometimes the technology becomes the focus, rather than the learning itself, and this is especially true when people are dazzled by technology just because it is impressive in itself – the 'gee-whiz factor'.

Rather than getting carried away with the marvels of the technology, you should look for ways the technology can make the learning experience better. This is the acid test: whether it can make the learning work better. If it can't, then no matter how clever the technology is, it is just not appropriate.

There is a kind of multiplier effect in play here whereby e-learning multiplies the effects of both good and bad learning design. This is because of its speed of implementation and uptake, and because of its scalability. Good design offers us the chance to add value. As Josef Albers puts it, 'In design sometimes one plus one equals three'.

Good technology can transform an ordinary learning experience into something extraordinary, but bad technology often simply helps to highlight poor learning design. You need to be prudent in choosing technologies that actually help, not hinder, what you are trying to do. You need to design-in the technology to fit the learning needs. And you need to maintain the perspective that it is there to serve the learning.

5. Exploiting the strengths of the web

The world wide web offers some of the richest media available today (certainly in comparison with other publishing contexts). It offers dynamic content such as video, audio and animation; great communication potential for both synchronous and asynchronous learning; and an ideal opportunity to coordinate and direct offline activities.

These are the strengths of the web, and should be used in effective e-learning design. A good e-learning programme is likely to include some or all of the following features: rich media, dynamic content, a communication facility and a focal point for a mixed-media (or blended) programme.

Many learners are used to encountering these media in their leisure uses of the web, including activities such as game playing and movie watching. It is important that learning offers an entertainment factor, and this has always been the case. For years, surveys conducted in the United Kingdom by the Industrial Society (now the Work Foundation) found that what learners valued most in face-to-face training sessions was not good content, or exchanging ideas with their peers, or even the competence of the trainer, but the *friendliness* of the trainer. And many facilitators will testify that the high scores on their evaluation sheets bear a direct relationship to how many laughs learners got during the course. Boredom and learning do not mix: you can have ineffective learning that entertains, but you will rarely find effective learning where there was no entertainment. The web is no different, but enjoys the advantage of media that lend themselves to having fun.

We can have e-learning, in its broadest sense, without using the web, instead just using corporate networks, or learning stored on a stand-alone hard drive, or on portable media such as CD ROMs and DVDs, but this is to miss out on some of the greatest opportunities.

LOOKING AT THE DIFFERENT MODELS

When you bear in mind all the good-practice experience, all the 'rules' and guidance about getting e-learning design right, I think some questions arise about the validity of rapid e-learning development. I understand that sometimes there are time pressures about putting something in place, but in most cases I am convinced that urgency should be subordinate to the need to do things properly and design an effective solution. (Of course, 'rapid' advocates would argue that rapid development does that, albeit using shortcuts.) This leads us into some practical considerations.

Beyond the five general principles, you will need a different design strategy for each model you use, but the design strategies for the first two models will be broadly similar. In both of these you are aiming to produce a course to be studied online. The only difference is that in the second model, this is combined with offline elements. Therefore, I shall recommend a broadly common approach to both models.

THE ROUTE MAP

When you design an online course, it sometimes helps to think of it as a journey to be taken by the learners, and to offer a route map to the learners to guide them along the way. Thus, as they progress through a series of pages, they should be following the road signs that show them each step along the way, and the final destination at the end of the route.

The metaphor of the signpost is powerful. Many designers of e-learning, and before that open and distance learning, have insisted on having good, clear signposting of learning paths.

We should beware the danger of copying design principles from other formats or other media; we need an approach specific to e-learning. Thus, for example, it does not work to constantly repeat the objectives set for learners, as in print-based open or distance learning. This seems too repetitive online, especially when you have the option to offer a hyperlink to a single location for the objectives.

The central idea of the route map is to separate the signposting of the route to be followed from the branches off the main route, the loops, lay-bys and side streets that feature the details learners have to absorb, and opportunities for them to test and discuss ideas. Thus, the 'branches off' include:

- *readings* (ideally given as PDFs or Word documents, or similar, unless they are very small);

- *resources*, such as presentations, simulations, sound clips and videos (anything mainly passive, just like readings);

- *activities*, such as discussions, games, simulations (the ones that require more active learner input, rather than just observation) and practical exercises (anything mainly active, requiring a high degree of learner input);

- *assessments* (of both formative and summative types, and of all formats).

This is illustrated in Figure 5.4.

All the branches ultimately converge, and thus there is more than one way of arriving at the destination, the end of the course. There will be many distractions along the branches, but the final destination will always be clear. Along the trunk route the pages will be deliberately sparse, including just headings, aims, instructions, key points, and illustrations of these, but nothing else. The bulk of the course content will lie in the branches.

For model 2, integrating online and offline learning, you have the additional consideration of how you make the links between online and

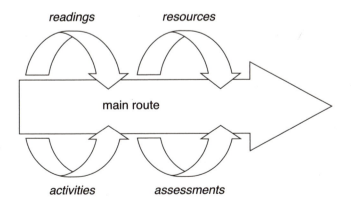

Figure 5.4 The route map

offline work. Seamless linking is vital, and in each case you need to make sure the learner feels motivated to switch from one mode to another.

The route map provides us with a tool to avoid the pitfalls of focus on content rather than process, of e-reading and of passivity. It effectively creates a design template to ensure consistency in design of online and blended courses.

DESIGNING LIVE E-LEARNING

In some respects the design of live e-learning is more akin to the design of traditional face-to-face learning activities, in that it seeks to replicate as far as possible a face-to-face experience in an online setting. This means there are fewer design issues of concern, but there are still guidelines to follow and pitfalls to avoid.

The facilitator, or organizer of the event, needs to ensure that he or she has access both to his or her own coordinating screen and to a screen that exactly replicates the learner's view. This may mean sitting in front of two PCs, but so be it; it's what is necessary to ensure you design and deliver a learner-centred experience.

Some thought needs to be given to the preparation for, and introduction to, the event, including issues such as establishing visual contact, checking sound levels (perhaps using test music), confirming connections, welcoming participants and providing information, perhaps as a rotation of presentation slides summarizing the objectives and what is to follow.

Attention needs to be given to the arrangement of objects on the screen, following the general web design issues discussed earlier in the chapter. One additional issue here is that the head-shot of the facilitator needs to be positioned centre-screen of the video frame, and the shot kept clear of any distracting background clutter.

Finally, the design should allow for a rapid start, getting into the substance of the event as quickly as possible, as this will be necessary to capture the attention of learners and get them quickly involved.

DESIGNING SELF-MANAGED LEARNING

Of all the e-learning models to provide design rules for, self-managed learning is the hardest, as it is so flexible in its nature that there can be lots of design options. The principles of good web design apply here, ensuring you have design features and layouts that facilitate ease of finding things, navigation, usability and so on. But beyond that, it depends what you want the site to do and how you want learners to use it. A more informal application means you can opt for a variety of different design approaches, while a more rigid application, such as to steer the learner through a continuous professional development (CPD) programme, may need to be more restrictive. In the latter case you probably need a design approach more like the route map for models 1 and 2.

The self-managed learning model is the one that usually best serves the needs of communities of practice (CoP). This is a particular approach, with design requirements of its own. Etienne Wenger's work on communities of practice pre-dates the development of e-learning, but it is only with e-learning that such communities can now be properly resourced to fulfil their learning needs. A CoP is a group of people with more than a shared interest in a subject (a community of interest); in a CoP the participants share in actually doing something. Examples would be people who work in the same industry, or professionals working in a particular geographical area, or academics working on a cross-institutional project.

Whether your self-managed learning is to support a CoP or to drive a CPD scheme, or is simply for informal learning, you need to bear in mind that it is an expression of knowledge management, and design it so that there are ample opportunities to create knowledge, to acquire it and to share it. After that, it is just a matter of getting the details right.

DESIGNING ELECTRONIC PERFORMANCE SUPPORT

Electronic performance support (EPS) is perhaps the least explored of the e-learning models, the one we have least experience of to provide lessons for new designs, far less a coherent theory. Perhaps the golden rule is that information in an EPS system should be readily available and easy to find – otherwise it will not be fit for purpose. But there has to be more to EPS; it has to offer more than just an electronic reference manual, or else it is just an information resource and does not merit being recognized as a model of e-learning.

I have not yet seen enough of EPS to say more than that the system must be capable of interrogation, must be capable of taking learner input about new problems or situations, and must offer interactivity for the learner. And, of course, in many cases it must be designed to ensure it can be accessed and put to best use from a handheld device, as that is how many learners will experience EPS in their places of work. I suspect EPS may work best when combined with model 2 to create wider opportunities to discuss work problems. We need pioneers in this field to record their experiences and contribute to the evolution of a new design theory.

MICRO-DESIGN

In closing this chapter I should like to offer a practical guide to how to design e-learning at the micro level – a list of the dos and don'ts of micro-design.

Do:

- include plenty of signposting: clear headings for objectives, section breaks, etc, consistent icons and other visual devices;
- offer simple navigation, including especially an 'in-your-face', obvious way of moving to the next page;
- find neat ways of organizing information: in menus, batteries of bullet points, checklists, tables, etc;
- use hyperlinks to connect to relevant points of comparison, further study, etc;
- deploy as many interactive features as possible (eg conceal-and-reveal);
- organize readings into separate sections (likewise video and audio clips);
- use a consistent colour scheme and consistent iconography;
- use colour to highlight things of importance;
- offer learners plenty of variety;
- present information pictorially wherever possible – the old saw that 'a picture is worth a thousand words' is only a slight exaggeration;
- use humour wherever possible;
- maintain simplicity wherever possible.

Don't:

- over-clutter (plenty of white space is a good thing!);
- include too much text on the screen;
- have pages that scroll beyond a standard screen size, unless absolutely necessary in the vertical plane, and almost never in the horizontal plane;

- deploy any feature in too large a format, as it slows down page loads (compress images, video and audio clips to the smallest size possible);

- use very small fonts;

- use colours that clash;

- over-complicate things;

- use design features without a reason – it's distracting;

- be culturally exclusive or offensive;

- be ambiguous;

- be repetitive;

- be boring.

Lastly, it cannot be emphasized enough that this is an evolving field. There may be plenty of design manuals, but too little thinking about e-learning has been about how we go about designing it, and about developing a theory of e-learning design. This chapter is one of the first attempts to construct such a theory, but there may be some way still to go. To borrow a phrase from Thomas Edison, 'There ain't no rules around here! We're trying to accomplish something.'

Illustrative project

The consultants suggested an approach that worked well for us. We had a few simple pages that guided the learner towards meeting the course objectives, then linked or attached learning resources off of these.

We used videos we still had from our old CD ROMs showing actual scenes in our stores and broke them into small clips, with review questions interspersed. We linked to relevant readings that already existed. We suggested exercises to try out at work, and brought the learners back to a reflection-and-feedback page. And we finished with assessment questions.

This format worked so well that we treated it as the template and designed all of our courses the same way, which made them easy to find your way around. After the first course, we didn't use the consultants any more, and just built each course ourselves. As we built more, we commissioned new content, including shooting new video (which was easier and much less expensive than we thought).

We found we could integrate these online courses with whatever offline support we wanted, varying it to suit local circumstances. And so we got the blended learning model we'd wanted all along.

SUMMARY OF KEY POINTS

1. Having a coherent and consistent approach to e-learning design is an essential part of having an e-learning strategy.

2. Design is one of the three component parts of e-learning, and the one that learning and development professionals can most directly influence to help ensure that e-learning is effective.

3. Design is important. It's about communicating effectively and facilitating more effective e-learning; it's not just about aesthetics.

4. There are two focuses in design: the learner, and the purpose of the learning. These, more than anything else, should determine the design strategy.

5. The five general principles of e-learning design are that it should be a managed programme; it should be an effective learning experience; it should be a learning process, not just e-reading; it should use technology to enhance learning; and it should exploit the strengths of the web.

6. The route map approach is the best way to design e-learning for models 1 and 2, and in some cases model 3. And there are useful design guidelines for all the models.

7. It is important to get the details right. It is important, too, to challenge design theory constantly. This is an evolving field where we do not yet have all the answers.

E-learning strategy: measurement and results

In this chapter we examine the strategic importance of e-learning evaluation, considering what we are trying to measure and why, and what results e-learning needs to produce. We identify five different approaches to e-learning evaluation, weigh up their strengths and weaknesses, and make recommendations on how to ensure e-learning delivers value.

MAKING A BUSINESS CASE

The fourth aspect of e-learning strategy, and also the fourth stage of the four-stage learning cycle (see Chapter 1), is evaluation; it's about how we measure the contribution of e-learning to establish whether it achieves the business outcomes, or results, we need. This ties in closely with Chapter 3, on strategy development and alignment, and with the issues of advocacy raised in Chapter 2: we need tools to help us construct a business case for e-learning, both taking a predictive look forward at what we want to implement, and looking back, historically, to review the merits of what we have done. In this respect, e-learning is no different from any other learning approach. All learning approaches should be subject to the same scrutiny.

Some learning and development professionals complain that learning always has to justify itself, while other business initiatives, such as e-mail, are taken for granted and not subjected to the same level of scrutiny. They feel they are constantly and unfairly under the spotlight. This is a little paranoid.

In my experience, any organization planning to implement e-mail put the plans through very rigorous scrutiny, and e-mail's proponents had to make a sound business case – as happens with any major investment. And that remains true for organizations changing over, say, from Lotus Notes to Microsoft Outlook. But after an initial technology investment there has been little recurring cost in running a corporate e-mail system, and the same should be true of e-learning.

We should expect to incur costs in establishing any new approach to learning: start-up costs, and putting in place the infrastructure, such as learning technology. But we should also expect the recurring costs to be greatly reduced if there is a significant upfront investment. And this is where vendors have let us down, because many of them have established systems to ensure annual recurring revenue streams for them (eg hosting, upgrades, software support and maintenance, etc). This is justifiable for providing new learning content and design, but for maintaining the technology it is just a rip-off. Vendors have been greedy, and this has distorted the market.

However, we still have to determine how we are going to evaluate e-learning, what measures we will put in place and what should be measured. This is an opportunity we should welcome. As Jack Welch says, 'An organization's ability to learn and translate that learning into action is the ultimate competitive advantage.' If we believe in learning, and e-learning, we should be confident about making our case.

FIVE DIFFERENT APPROACHES

In the broadest terms, evaluation may be described as the systematic determination of the merit, worth or significance of something or someone. In learning and development, including e-learning, the determination of the 'merit', 'worth' or 'significance' is in terms of what learners have learned and can apply at work, and what that means for their organizations.

Evaluation is a diverse discipline embracing many qualitative and quantitative methods. A brief web search yielded the following list: accelerated ageing, action research, advanced product quality planning, alternative assessment, appreciative inquiry, assessment, axiomatic design, Baldrige criteria, Balanced Scorecard, benchmarking, book-keeping, case study, change management, clinical trial, cohort study, competency, competitor analysis, consensus decision-making, consensus-seeking decision-making, content analysis, conversation analysis, cost–benefit analysis, critical path analysis, data mining, Delphi technique, discourse analysis, educational accreditation, environmental scanning, ethnography, experiment, experimental techniques, factor analysis, factorial experiment, feasibility study, field experiment, fixtureless in-circuit test, focus group, force field analysis, game theory, grading, historical method, immanent evaluation, inquiry, interview, Kirkpatrick's four levels, marketing research, meta-analysis, metrics, most significant change, multivariate statistics, naturalistic observation, observational techniques, opinion polling, organizational learning, Outcome Mapping, participant observation, Participatory Impact Pathways Analysis, policy analysis, portfolios and electronic portfolios, Program Evaluation and Review Technique (PERT), process improvement, project management, qualitative research, quality assurance, quality audit, quality circle, quality control, quality management, quantitative research, questionnaire, questionnaire construction, Return on Expectation, Return on Investment, root cause analysis, rubrics, sampling, self-assessment, Six Sigma, standardized testing, statistical process analysis and control, statistical survey, statistics, strategic planning, structured interviewing, systems theory, student testing, survey research, Total Quality Management, total value-add and triangulation. This is by no means exhaustive, and arguably all, or nearly all, of these methods have their place in evaluating learning and development. To make any sense of this, we need to be able to narrow it down and classify this feast of techniques into something more digestible.

There are broadly five sets of approaches to evaluation from the above list that are in more or less common use, none of which is entirely exclusive of the others, and all of which have merit. There may indeed be others, but we shall focus on these five as they offer a range of philosophies and practical techniques to suit most tastes and conceivable circumstances. We shall examine each of them in turn, consider their relevance and effectiveness, and try to judge whether e-learning has any special affinity with them. Then we shall attempt to draw some conclusions.

The five are:

- Kirkpatrick's four levels;

- return on investment (ROI);

- return on expectation (ROE);

- Six Sigma;

- total value-add.

KIRKPATRICK'S FOUR LEVELS

For many years, the 'gold standard' in evaluation of learning and development has been Donald Kirkpatrick's four levels: reactions, learning, behaviour and results. Many trainers know little or nothing else. See Figure 6.1.

Kirkpatrick's enduring idea, originating in 1959, was not just to distinguish the four levels, but to demonstrate that you can consider the impact of all training activities at each of these levels. Kirkpatrick described these as four levels, rather than simply four discrete areas of measurement, because they form a hierarchy (as in Figure 6.1) in which each successive level benefits from information gathered at the level below.

The *reactions* level is about gauging what learners think and feel, and is usually conducted at the end of a piece of learning. This can be done very informally, and a good trainer will always seek to elicit some verbal feedback, but the most common method is getting learners to fill in a form. Some commentators deride such a form as a 'happy sheet', as it merely tells you how happy the learners are and not very much else (and arguably it tends to yield favourable, or 'happy', results regardless of whether learners are actually satisfied). But reactions are the easiest of the levels to measure, and this is especially true of online courses, where a short questionnaire can be tagged on to the end of any course or module.

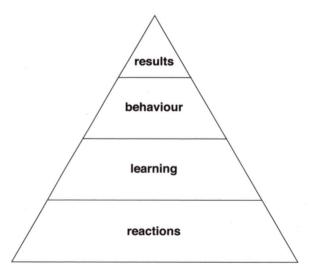

Figure 6.1 Kirkpatrick's four levels

The *learning* level is about measuring what learners have actually absorbed in terms of new knowledge, expertise or perhaps to some extent capability or competence. This is what academic examinations do, and it is what trainers can measure by setting tests, including practical tests and simulations. In formal education this is the last, and most important, level, as it shows whether an academic course has done what it set out to achieve in terms of pass rates. In learning for work, the issue is a little more complex, hence the levels to follow. But this level is still important. In e-learning it is relatively easy to set quizzes and more formal assessments online, although (as we saw in Chapter 4) there are limitations to what can be automatically assessed.

The *behaviour* level is about looking beyond what learners attain in terms of course marks, and measuring what has changed in terms of their behaviour at work. It is about the skills employees can demonstrate, as distinct from those employees' skill levels pre-training; it is about their ability to perform tasks required in their job; it is about their competence; and it is about bringing out the best of their strengths and talents. So if the object of a learning intervention is to make someone a better manager, this level is the true measure of the success of the course, regardless of whether he or she passed the exam (the learning level). It is how the person now does the job that counts.

Like a traditional course, e-learning cannot actually offer this measure in itself – what it can do is simulate work conditions – but e-learning can be so designed that it aims to optimize learning transfer and subsequent employee performance. In this it is no different from other approaches to learning.

The *results* level is about the wider consequences of the learning, the gains for the organization. This, ultimately, is the whole point of learning and development: achieving business results. The gains could arise from anything: improving sales or profits, cutting waste, regulatory or contract compliance, or environmental improvements. This level is often the hardest to measure, and therefore is the level that tends to be measured least, but, as many point out, it is the most important level of all. This remains as true for e-learning as for any other approach. E-learning's advantage may lie in its capacity to build in automated information gathering to help show improved results.

Kirkpatrick's four levels are a tried and tested approach to evaluation and can be as readily applied to e-learning as to any other learning and development. However, essentially they are just a framework within which you can position whatever other tools and techniques you wish. The development of other approaches has arisen less from concerns about any inherent weakness in Kirkpatrick than from a desire to exploit other techniques and perhaps find something more. Advocates of other approaches are often critical of Kirkpatrick, but often this seems to be just to provide justification for trying another route.

A simple application of the Kirkpatrick levels to e-learning would mean including an online evaluation sheet at the end of each online course; providing an online summative assessment exercise at the end of each course; getting learners to input their responses to a pre-course survey of their skills or competence prior to taking the online course and then following up with a post-course survey to yield a before-and-after comparison; and, finally, setting an initial target, pulling together all the data from the foregoing, and measuring performance in relation to the pre-set target. Of course, more sophisticated, and more imaginative, applications are also possible.

The 'before and after' formula may be applied in most evaluation approaches, and with good reason: it's a reality check. As George Bernard Shaw famously remarked, 'The only man who behaves sensibly is my tailor; he takes my measurements anew every time he sees me, while all the rest go on with their old measurements and expect me to fit them.'

RETURN ON INVESTMENT

Some say there is a fifth level, beyond results, and that this is return on investment (ROI). Since the 1990s, leading US commentator Jack Phillips has been perhaps the foremost exponent of this idea. I think it derives from a mistaken, restrictive interpretation of the results level, and a more understandable wish to emphasize the ultimate benefits for the organization. In contradistinction, I would say that ROI is a means of measuring the fourth level.

Some of ROI's strongest advocates argue that most of what is measured in the name of learning evaluation, inclusive of all of the Kirkpatrick levels, is to do with the efficiency of the learning and development function, which, although worthwhile, is much less significant than the returns for the business, an effectiveness measure. This is fair enough, but it does not prove that ROI is a fifth level. So, let's look at what it really is.

The core idea of ROI is to measure, in financial terms, the benefits to the business, which are essentially the increases in business income, *minus* the actual costs of offering the learning. This applies to everything in business, not just learning, and the equation is that the return on investment equals the ratio of money gained or lost on an investment to the amount of money invested. When we apply this to e-learning, it reveals the percentage return you make over a specified period as a result of investing in e-learning. The basic formula for this is shown in Figure 6.2.

$$\frac{\text{Total benefits}}{\text{Total costs}} = \text{ROI}$$

Figure 6.2 ROI formula

Cost–benefit analysis, which is essentially what this is, underpins many business decisions: you identify and add up the benefits, you identify and subtract the costs, and you arrive at a measure of your return. In the above formula, by using division rather than subtraction we arrive at a result that may then be expressed as a percentage.

But this is an oversimplification. Many benefits and costs are difficult to identify, let alone measure, and this leads to approximations, guesswork, margins for error, and skewed results. Experienced business leaders are well aware of these problems and the scope they allow for overenthusiastic suppliers or subordinates to distort the picture. This has led to widespread scepticism about how genuine a measure ROI is, in real life, and a tired cynicism that it can be used to prove any case.

The other critical variable is time. There is no point in proving that an e-learning programme will achieve great benefits after five years if the costs all have to be sustained in the first two years and nobody knows whether these benefits will still be important five years into the future. A famous, often-quoted example of the benefit of e-learning comes from Cisco, which found that it took more than six months to roll out new-product training for its global sales force – but the snag with this was that new products had a life cycle of less than six months before they were superseded by new, improved products, so even before the training was complete it was as obsolete as the product. E-learning overcame the time barrier in this example, but time remains a problem in many others.

The simple tool most businesses use to measure ROI against time is *payback*. This measures how long it takes for the benefits to overtake the costs, and thus yields a payback period, or the time it takes to break even on an investment.

But the larger the investment and the longer the period of time involved, the less accurate payback becomes. Accountants view payback as a very crude measure, and seek more reliable but more complex calculation approaches, such as the internal rate of return (IRR) method or the accounting rate of return (ARR) method, or discounted cash flow (DCF) return. Each of these takes account, in various ways, of factors such as depreciation, allowance for inflation, opportunity cost of alternative investments, accounting conventions, etc.

The most sophisticated and most highly regarded of these methods is *net present value* (NPV). With NPV, effectively the return is adjusted to take account of capital depreciation, interest, vagaries of the firm's accounting practices and, perhaps most importantly, the effects of inflation. This means that a projected return, when looking ahead, is expressed in present-day values, or in other words adjusted to take account of the effects of inflation (a retrospective calculation will use the actual rates of inflation). NPV is a useful business tool but only where the scale of investment justifies such a major effort of evaluation (in itself costly and time-consuming), and many businesses that recognize the accuracy of NPV still prefer simple payback for working purposes.

When calculating ROI for a traditional training course, you need to take account of costs such as trainers' salaries and expenses; hire of facilities and equipment; external training providers' fees; administration costs; promotional costs; travel, accommodation and subsistence; and the salaries, as a measure of the lost work time, of the learners. There will be plenty of others, depending on circumstances, and to give a true account no stone should be left unturned in identifying and calculating all costs. The benefits may be classified under headings such as labour savings, productivity increases, cost savings and waste reduction. Specific benefits will depend on the circumstances of your organization, but will certainly need to be defined more narrowly to reach accurate measurements and to make a convincing business case.

When you are calculating ROI for an e-learning intervention, the costs may include the following: technology investment, perhaps upgrading the corporate ICT network, or user terminals; implementing a specific e-learning application such as a VLE, including licence fees, hosting, software support and maintenance; development or adaptation of e-learning content; and many of the same costs as for a traditional training course. The benefits will be broadly the same as in the preceding example, but again you should spell out the specifics in your situation.

The great strength of ROI is that is yields tangible measures in pure financial terms, speaking a language that business leaders understand. Its weakness is that it represents a *reductio ad absurdum*, evading some of the more complicated, yet vitally important, issues in learning for work. It has been criticized for encouraging short-termism, because of the pressure to show ROI over the shortest possible payback period. It has other problems too: What do you choose to measure, how do you measure it, and over what period? How do you deal with the cynicism that there are lies, damned lies, statistics and ROI? And how do you take account of the aspects of learning that defy measurement, or of the unexpected things that take you by surprise in the learning process? These problems have led to investigation of other evaluation approaches.

RETURN ON EXPECTATION

ROI starts from the assumption that everyone shares the same business language – the language of the balance sheet – and that that value can be expressed in financial terms that everyone can agree with. That is usually a safe bet, but return on expectation (ROE) challenges this fundamental assumption.

In their influential book *The HR Value Proposition*, Dave Ulrich and Wayne Brockbank contend that:

> Value is defined by the receivers of HR work – the investors, customers, line managers, and employers – more than by the givers. HR is successful if and when its stakeholders perceive that it produces value. Delivering what matters most to stakeholders focuses on the deliverables (outcomes of HR) rather than on the doables (activities of HR).

While the last sentence has an echo of the ROI argument about focusing on effectiveness rather than efficiency, on the business results rather than the housekeeping, this is a very different philosophy from ROI – and one that cannot be wholly explained by the different perspectives suggested by the examples. ROI advocates often sound as though they are thinking like learning providers or consultants, while Ulrich and Brockbank seem to see ROE through the spectacles of the corporate HR or learning and development manager.

The fundamental principle underpinning ROE is that you need to define the value (which may or may not be capable of being reduced to a financial measure), the value that your customers are looking for, and aim to deliver that value, which means conducting some before-and-after measurements. A growing company that routinely delivers year-on-year sales-figure increases may not be particularly impressed by learning outcomes that add one or two percentage points to the top line, but its managers may be extremely excited by learning outcomes that yield a tiny – beyond the decimal point – percentage increase to profits on existing sales, as this makes a much bigger difference to the company's bottom line. This example shows that clarifying expectations can make a significant difference.

In the United Kingdom the CIPD took a lead in this in 2007 when it commissioned and published research by Dr Valerie Anderson and the University of Portsmouth Business School into the value of learning, and published an accompanying book by Anderson. Anderson and colleagues characterize ROI as a 'one-size-fits-all' approach and strongly advocate a focus on understanding value and meeting expectations instead.

Clearly, this means the expectations to be met will vary from situation to situation, but Anderson and colleagues identified four common factors that influence how learning is valued:

- senior management's trust in the learning contribution;

- the organization's need for learning-value metrics;

- the strategic significance of short-term capability requirements;

- the strategic significance of long-term capability requirements.

The report recommended that organizations should use these themes to begin the process of clarifying precisely what value means for them.

While ROE is a different approach, it remains compatible with ROI. Some use the term TROI, meaning True ROI, as an alternative to ROE essentially meaning the same thing: that the ROI has to be pre-matched to the needs and expectations of the learners and their managers, the business and its customers. The Anderson report concluded that there are four sets of measurement and reporting needed (which makes a nice contrast with the Kirkpatrick four levels). These are:

- learning function efficiency measures;

- key performance indicators and benchmark measures;

- ROI measures;

- ROE measures.

Thus, there are clear indications as to how an organization could synthesize the approaches.

SIX SIGMA

A similar theme to ROE is present in the genesis of the Six Sigma approach to learning – and e-learning – evaluation, in that there is recognition of a need to take the perspective of the users of learning's outcomes. Six Sigma advocates argue that business measures, not training measures, are needed to capture the imagination of learning's customers. Six Sigma has a different philosophical foundation in that it sets out to identify and remove the causes of defects and errors, rather than simply to measure success. The adoption of Six Sigma by Jack Welch when he was CEO of General Electric led to a wider popularization of the technique, and some claim that it is now used, or has been used, by more than two-thirds of the world's leading companies.

Six Sigma is a registered service mark and a trademark of Motorola Incorporated. One of the company's engineers, Bill Smith, is credited with inventing the methodology in 1986, although its advocates can trace its history further back – even to the 18th century. Sigma is the Greek letter that, for statisticians, symbolizes standard deviation, a measure of variation; the number six derives from the number of process steps required to produce the Six Sigma goal of fewer than 3.4 defects (variations from the accepted standard) per million opportunities. Hence, Six Sigma is the process whereby organizations improve quality by eliminating as far as possible deviations from the required norm. Motorola claims over $17 billion in savings in its first 20 years of implementing the process, and it is the cornerstone of Motorola University, widely recognized as the first corporate university in the world.

Why 3.4 defects per million? Sometimes people talk glibly of 99 per cent accuracy as though this is an acceptable level, but in almost any business application it is not. One customer complaint out of every hundred customer interactions is a lot to deal with, especially for a business dealing with a mass consumer base running into hundreds of thousands; and in dangerous work, one fatality for every hundred employees is clearly an unacceptable level of accidental deaths. The figure of 3.4 defects in a million instances derives from the statistical improvements achievable at each Sigma level up to six, and equates to 99.999 per cent accuracy, a far higher standard.

The application of Six Sigma to learning and development has been championed by Kaliym Islam in his work at the Depository Trust and Clearing Corporation (DTCC) in the United States and in his book *Developing and Measuring Training the 6 Sigma Way*, which includes a case study of implementing e-learning the Six Sigma way at DTCC. Islam decries the instructional system design (ISD) approach – widely recognized terminology in the United States, but not really elsewhere – as divorced from business reality, and criticizes its theoretical forebears, including Donald Kirkpatrick, as ivory-tower academics lacking business acumen.

The concept of ISD, especially the term 'instruction', jars with those of us who prefer learner-centred learning (see Chapter 2), as does Islam's preference for discussing training rather than learning. It looks to me as though the expressions of learning and development he has worked with are of the old, didactic style, and while his critique of that is more than justified, his conclusion of the need for Six Sigma represents a leap of logic given that other approaches address the same issues and are just as valid.

Islam recommends a model of Six Sigma called DMADDI, which he describes in six phases: Define, Measure, Analyse, Design, Develop and Implement; this is represented in Table 6.1.

At the end of each phase in this process a 'tollgate' review takes place, ensuring that the learning remains on track to fulfil business expectations, represented as the 'voice of the business' and the 'voice of the customer'. With Six Sigma, evaluation becomes an activity integrated with the rest of the learning or e-learning strategy. It becomes connected with the language and culture of the business. And it should become not just more efficient but more effective.

There are broad criticisms of Six Sigma. It is generally recognized as effective at what it is intended to do, but its focus is on fixing existing processes, which does not help in identifying new products, services or processes, or in responding to changing circumstances. In other words, it is more to do with efficiency than with effectiveness. It has been alleged that it can stifle creativity. It is also open to the criticism, as with NPV for ROI, that the investment needed in it is disproportionate to the gains it measures, although with Six Sigma this may be only a start-up phenomenon, as once the process is embedded, it should become part of the furniture. It seems to be well suited to manufacturing, where it originated, and has transferred well to industries, such as financial services where there are clear processes to follow. Whether it is such a good fit beyond these industries is open to question. I would argue that learning and

Table 6.1 DMADDI for Six Sigma

Phase	*Description*
Define	What are the business requirements?
Measure	What targets do we need to meet?
Analyse	What needs to be learned?
Design	How should we teach it?
Develop	Does our prototype match our design?
Implement	Did the implementation meet business and instructional requirements?

development in general, and most models of e-learning in particular, lie beyond its scope. However, learning and development professionals working in these industries may find a cultural affinity that steers them towards it.

TOTAL VALUE-ADD

Many gains for a business can be hard to measure in financial terms. Marketing professionals have a saying that half of their advertising budget is wasted; they just don't know which half. This is an admission that they are doing something they are sure is of value, but find it hard to make a definitive justification based on the bottom line. Similarly, some aspects of a business, such as brand values or customer goodwill, are very difficult to place a monetary value on in the balance sheet. Even so, there is general agreement that they have some value, perhaps considerable value, although whatever figure is included is a matter of guesswork. Over-optimistic guessing lay behind the dotcom boom-and-bust around the turn of the millennium.

Let's consider another set of examples. Sometimes learning and development activities, including e-learning, can have an indirect goal, such as the example in the strategic alignment section of Chapter 3 of a company encouraging closer cooperation between employees in different locations. In that example, the cooperation would be expected to lead to bottom-line benefits later on, but as an end in itself would have no financial benefit. Another example would be managing diversity to ensure equal opportunities for all employees regardless of sex, ethnic origin or other diversities. This could be to maximize employee performance and make gains in the future, but again, it would have no financial benefit as a direct result in the short term. Encouraging employees to develop the learning habit comes into the same category; enlightened companies realize that if their employees are keen to learn, it will be easier to implement change when required.

In short, there are many instances where gains to be made from e-learning, other learning interventions or a range of other business activities may be difficult or impossible to measure in financial terms.

Since the 1990s, businesses have increasingly become aware of their intellectual capital. This may be the most significant 'intangible' measure of business value yet. Intellectual capital, to quote Patrick Sullivan, is

> the sum of a firm's ideas, inventions, technologies, general knowledge, computer programs, designs, data skills, processes, creativity, and

publications... intellectual capital is knowledge that can be converted into profits.

Business managers and accountants are forever trying to quantify these assets, adding them to annual reports, while independent business analysts are forever extracting them as unreliable as they try to define a company's true value for investors. Yet everyone knows there is something very important going on here.

In his magnum opus, *Intellectual Capital*, Thomas Stewart sets out to show that the most important measures of value in a business are its knowledge assets, and that the strategic development and deployment of these assets is the key to lasting competitive advantage, now and in the future. Stewart caricatures the work of corporate accountants as counting the bottles rather than describing the wine, and insists that it is the latter sort of value that is the hidden gold of organizations. Sullivan, Stewart and others argue that knowledge management is a process, perhaps the key process, for achieving sustainable business growth, but they cannot always prove it in dollars and cents.

What all of this – advertising, brand value, goodwill, indirect benefits, intellectual capital and more – bears witness to is the simple truth that not everything can be reduced to a financial measure, and this is as true of learning and development as of anything else. This leads us to the conclusion that our evaluation of e-learning needs to embrace not just the financial return on our investment but an all-encompassing evaluation of all value added.

As Kevin Kruse puts it, 'ROI analysis effectively minimizes the risk of failures and financial waste, but it also reduces the chance for innovative breakthroughs and tough-to-measure results. By only focusing on ROI, [you] may miss some tremendous opportunities to contribute to [your] organization's strategic goals.' To be clear, Kruse does not advocate turning your back on ROI, but rather believes that it should be only one part of the overall business case. As a side note, this critique of ROI could equally be applied to Six Sigma.

Kruse also advocates the acronym CASE when considering total value add for e-learning projects. The initials represent the four main areas Kruse recommends you should bear in mind when looking for value: **C**ontent, **A**utomation of process, **S**ynchronous learning and **E**xperimentation. You may be able to identify further fields; the point is that total value-add demands a wider lens and seeks to encompass much more than narrower measures such as ROI.

Total value-add is thus about using the ROE technique of clarifying what sort of value is most desired, about using ROI measures as well as others, and about building the case for e-learning on the accumulation of all the value it adds.

IS E-LEARNING DIFFERENT?

Most of what we have discussed in this chapter applies equally to all learning and development, not just e-learning. The five approaches we have described in some detail are applicable to all learning and development; indeed, ROI, ROE, Six Sigma and total value-add are applicable to all business activities. So, in this sense, there is nothing really different about e-learning.

Nevertheless, we should consider the specific characteristics of e-learning, not just our own corporate cultures, when choosing an evaluation approach, and try to come up with a best fit. And we should be certain that our chosen approach fits with our e-learning strategy.

My preference is for a total value-add approach, but I would resist any blueprint for evaluation, and recommend as strong a focus on the needs of the customers for our learning outcomes as we have a focus on crafting e-learning to the needs of the learners.

You need to bear in mind the distinction between making a business case as part of the process of advocacy for e-learning, and the use of the business case and evaluation in measuring the results and impact of learning. This distinction is between prediction of the future, and measuring and learning from the past. It is about moving from partisan advocacy of e-learning – fighting your corner – to objective calculation of exactly what gains the business has made. The following checklist should help you maintain this perspective.

AN EVALUATION CHECKLIST

1. Be clear in your own mind, and in all your communication, about the differences between evaluations at the four levels identified by Kirkpatrick.

2. Be clear about what your e-learning is supposed to achieve, not just for the learners but for the organization as a whole.

3. Be sensitive to the culture of your organization when choosing an evaluation approach.

4. Ensure that evaluation is an integral part of your e-learning strategy.

5. Ensure that your learning objectives link directly to business objectives.

6. Clarify the expectations of your key stakeholders, especially including your customers, *before* choosing your evaluation approach.

7. Make a business case that is clear about all kinds of value added, so that the overall contribution of e-learning is clear.

8. Be open and honest in measuring all the costs and benefits of learning. This is vital for the credibility of your evaluation, and your e-learning strategy as a whole.

By approaching evaluation in this way, we can ensure that it is inextricably linked with the other essential parts of our e-learning strategy: our strategy is developed with a view to the results it should achieve; our suppliers and resources are marshalled in such a way as to maximize potential and achieve these results; and our e-learning is designed not only to engage learners but also to contribute to these same results. This strategic approach to evaluation – measurement and results – fulfils a unity of purpose for our e-learning, which is what makes it successful.

A recurring theme in our evaluation checklist is about your behaviour, about what you do. This is akin to the thinking of economists on the factors of production, which has sought to add to the basic list of three factors (land, labour and capital) a crucial fourth factor that acts upon the others: the entrepreneur. Similarly, what binds together the four threads of our e-learning strategy – its development, the management of suppliers and resources, the e-learning design, and the evaluation – is the learning and development professional who drives it. This leads us into our last chapter.

Illustrative project

When I showed my e-learning strategy to the HR Director to get his feedback, his main criticism was that I hadn't addressed the issue of measurement, which senior management had emphasized.

I had been using everything from evaluation sheets to ROI calculations to show gains from our training programmes, but he wanted something more ambitious, and suggested we show Total Value Add from e-learning. This was a new idea to me, but the HR Director explained that we could identify more benefits from our e-learning than just the financial gains. Together we identified the atti-

tude shifts the business was trying to foster, and what signs of those we should look for, and we identified meausres of how the business could tap into employees' enthusiasm for digital technology and make more of our own digital investments.

When we implemented this, we were able to show not just a return on our investment, but a number of other strategic gains for the business – thanks to our e-learning programme.

SUMMARY OF KEY POINTS

1. Evaluation is one of the four stages of the training cycle, following needs analysis, planning and preparation, and delivery; and one of the four essential elements of an e-learning strategy, along with strategy development, managing suppliers and resources, and design issues.

2. There are five main approaches to the evaluation of e-learning: Kirkpatrick's four levels, return on investment (ROI), return on expectations (ROE), Six Sigma, and total value-add.

3. Kirkpatrick's four levels – reactions, learning, behaviour and results – provide a long-standing contextual framework for understanding e-learning evaluation.

4. ROI describes the range of means of measuring the ratio of e-learning's costs to its benefits, and the returns it yields to organizations, in financial terms.

5. ROE is about recognizing that value is defined by the customer and adjusting your evaluation strategy to meet this.

6. Six Sigma is a process for measuring the value of e-learning in terms that are meaningful to the business.

7. Total value-add describes the approach of recognizing all the different kinds of value e-learning can offer and ensuring that that contribution is recorded and recognized.

8. All these evaluation approaches may be applied to e-learning. Most of them are compatible, and your choice should be made on the basis of the best fit for your organization.

7

Learning more about e-learning

The preceding chapters have looked at e-learning strategy, and its successful implementation, in several dimensions, and now we focus in on the person at the centre of all of them – you. This chapter is rather more than an annotated bibliography. It draws on my personal experience and industry anecdotes, summarizes the sources used in this book and suggests a number of ways you can further your own personal development and learn more about e-learning.

PERSONAL EXPERIENCE

I was at a conference of e-learning practitioners a few years ago where Elliott Masie asked for a show of hands for who had undertaken e-learning in the past year. Very few hands went up. Then he asked who had undertaken a Google search in the past *week*. Nearly every hand went up. 'That's e-learning,' he claimed.

He was right, in a way. What the sea of hands attested to was use of the web for personal research and learning, or an informal version of model 3: self-managed e-learning. At the time, there were murmurings, as though this was a confidence trick. Most people would have recognized e-learning as models 1 or 2 and doubted that their experiences amounted to the same thing.

They were right, too. They had experienced one method, or one model, of e-learning, but the overwhelming majority had little or no experience of other methods. And this has been a significant problem for the growth of e-learning. In Chapter 1 we noted that too few learners had experience of more than one model, and this has distorted their view, especially with nobody pointing out that there are other models. It is much more damaging that learning and development professionals have the same limited experience.

I worked for several years in the field of open, flexible and distance learning (before these approaches benefited from electronic enhancement), and most people I worked with had experience of using these media and experiencing these approaches *as learners*. The user's perspective is critical: everyone thinks they know something about learning because we all learn all the time, and we have all experienced formal learning of some sort. But how many e-learning advocates have been on the receiving end of e-learning? Like Elliott Masie, I find remarkably few.

This needs to change. The first and most significant step learning and development professionals can take to enhance their understanding of e-learning is to become learners themselves and to try out all the e-learning models. This should be very easy. Most of us have already tried model 3, informal e-learning; those who have not should investigate Wikiversity (see below). There are plenty of free model 1 courses (of varying quality) to be found by a simple web search; and many vendors offer free webinars for model 4, live e-learning. This means the only models that are likely to require investment of funds as well as time are model 2, blended learning, and model 5, EPS. I would urge every learning and development professional to gain this experience, if they have not already done so, as a matter of priority. As George Santayana said, 'The wisest mind has something yet to learn.'

SELF-DEVELOPMENT

In devising your e-learning strategy and setting out to implement e-learning, you should consider your own capabilities to do so. A good starting point is to measure where you are now. I have provided two grids that may be used to assess and record your knowledge (Table 7.1) and experience (Table 7.2) of e-learning. You could fill them in yourself and/or invite colleagues who know your work to fill them in about you. You may want to add further areas of knowledge or experience to the lists in the left-hand columns.

After reading this book, you should be able at least to tick all the boxes in the middle column of the knowledge grid.

Table 7.1 Assessing and recording your knowledge of e-learning

What knowledge do you have of the following	*Little or none*	*Some*	*A great deal*
different e-learning models			
criteria for choosing an e-learning approach			
virtual learning environments			
authoring tools			
the range of specialist software available			
e-learning design principles			
ways of supporting e-learning			
e-assessment			
quality-assuring e-learning			
methods for evaluating e-learning			

Once you decide what you need to develop further, you should find plenty of scope for personal development through short courses, conferences and events, books and journals, and online communities. You can also pursue qualifications in e-learning: in the United Kingdom there are qualifications from awarding bodies such as the CIPD, the Institute of IT Training and the Scottish Qualifications Authority. All over the world there are many courses leading to qualifications from universities, colleges and private training providers.

However, this raises the question of whether there should be discrete qualifications in e-learning. On the whole, I think not. There is some specialist knowledge in the field (hence books like this) and there are some specific skills too. But the relevant ones could be incorporated into comprehensive learning and development qualifications, many of which are well established, while the less relevant ones, such as use of software applications, should be part of ICT qualifications. Perhaps broader qualifications could include modules on e-learning, although I accept that that is rather close to having separate qualifications anyway.

There is no internationally recognized standard, so there is no 'killer' qualification (like, say, the MBA for management), and I do not see one emerging in the near future. If this encourages creativity and more

Table 7.2 Assessing and recording your experience of e-learning

How would you describe your experience of the following	*Novice*	*Practitioner*	*Expert*
planning and managing e-learning			
designing an e-learning programme			
selecting and managing e-learning suppliers			
using a virtual environment			
using authoring tools			
using specialist software			
tutoring e-learners			
coaching or mentoring e-learners			
implementing e-assessment			
evaluating e-learning			

imaginative personal development on the part of e-learning practitioners, then that seems to me a good thing.

A SOURCE OF FURTHER LEARNING

By definition, learning and development professionals know a great deal about learning and development but not necessarily about digital technology. As when any other specialist field of knowledge comes into contact with our own, there is an obvious way to remedy our knowledge shortfall: engage with those who know more. In the case of e-learning, this means engaging with software vendors and other technology experts.

This book contains a number of serious criticisms of e-learning vendors, but the fact remains that they are experts in programming, software development and application, and as such have much to offer us. As we have noted, their attempts at learning applications so far leave a lot to be desired, but if they are prepared to engage with the learning and development profession openly and honestly, and without defending their past mistakes, then they could – and should – represent a valuable resource.

So, the action points for learning and development professionals are:

- Find ways to learn more about digital technology in general. Increase your store of knowledge, and look for ways technology can help learning.

- Find sympathetic e-learning vendors, engage with them, and work together to find new ways for technology to help learning.

Some might argue that this is what has happened already. Perhaps it has, to some extent at least. But the techies have been allowed to lead, and the ignorance and lack of confidence of learning and development professionals has helped them lead us up a cul-de-sac. We need a new approach. E-learning vendors do not want to be part of the problem; our challenge is to find ways to make them part of the solution.

GENERAL REFERENCE

Now I want to consider each of the chapters of this book in turn, comment on the sources and references for each of them, and suggest places to look to learn more. This represents almost a literature review for the subject of e-learning, but with the caveat that many titles from the beginnings of e-learning (1997 onwards) are now so dated as to be almost redundant. I also wish to point readers towards relevant sources beyond the field of e-learning.

I have consulted many titles in researching and writing this book, and a number of them offer valuable lessons for the general reader who wishes to know more about e-learning. There are also a number of more broadly useful books about learning and development, and about the wider subject of business strategy. Then there are the web references, which are by their nature not always as permanent as works in print but which I have tried to guide the reader to, wherever possible. The rest of this chapter tries to assemble them, with comments, into a sensible order.

LEARNING IN THE DIGITAL AGE

In the Introduction, I said that e-learning was still in vogue in many organizations. Perhaps that was wishful thinking on my part. There is certainly a lot less theorizing about e-learning around than there was 10 or even 5 years ago. On a visit to my nearest city-centre Borders bookshop in the spring of 2008 I failed to find a single book about e-learning on the shelves. I found plenty on other business subjects that I'm happy to report are 'still in vogue', including leadership, change, project management, Six Sigma, and even coaching and knowledge management. But if I wanted a book on e-learning, I should have had to order it (I didn't – they are cheaper online).

Specific web references given in this book were accessed during the spring and summer of 2008, and were available at that time. If by the time you read this they have moved, then hopefully the home page of the relevant site can help direct you to the new location. If they have gone altogether, perhaps a general web search will find them, or similar or related references, elsewhere. With some of the more ephemeral web content I have found Google's cache function helpful. Pages that no longer exist in their original locations are sometimes cached by Google. When a Google search yields the result you are looking for but the page can no longer be found, instead of clicking on the main link, choose the Google 'Cached' link, which may be found on the bottom line of the entry summary. Good luck.

Every so often, a business book comes along that catches the Zeitgeist. David Pottruck and Terry Pearce's *Clicks and Mortar* (Jossey-Bass, San Francisco, 2000) was almost the bible of e-business and the dotcom boom, and still resonates with its key message about the importance of people over technology. More recently we have *Wikinomics: How mass collaboration changes everything* by Don Tapscott and Anthony Williams (Penguin, London, 2007) and the accompanying website, http://www.wikinomics.com. Even if its conclusion seems over the top – 'The immutable, standalone Website is dead. Say hello to the Web that increasingly looks like a library full of chatty components that interact and talk to one another' – its central thesis of a new web-based economy based on user participation and collaboration seems right on the money. This is a valuable theoretical foundation to, among other things, the use of wikis and other collaborative tools for e-learning.

Understanding wikis is one of the keys to understanding how to make the most of the web, which in turn is one of the keys to understanding the digital age. So the obvious place to start is with the Wiki family of sites, notably Wikipedia, Wikiversity and Wikisource; http://en.wikipedia.org is an invaluable reference (icons linking to the other sites in the Wiki family may be found at the bottom of the page), and most of the concepts in this book can be checked against Wikipedia entries, sometimes incredibly extensive ones. There are other online encyclopedias, of course, such as Britannica and Encarta, but Wikipedia is rapidly outgrowing them all.

Links for further information about specific technologies, including Moodle and other open-source platforms, are given in the section on suppliers and resources, below.

Readers interested in finding out more about the work of the members of our Virtual Round Table may find good places to start at the following:

- Marius Meyer at http://www.unisa.ac.za

- Nigel Paine at http://www.nigelpaine.com

- Serge Ravet at http://www.eife-l.org

- Dr Allison Rossett at http://edweb.sdsu.edu/people/ARossett/ Arossett.html

- Martyn Sloman at http://www.cipd.co.uk (but please note that Martyn is due to leave CIPD in 2009 to take up a visiting fellowship at the University of Christchurch, New Zealand, and is likely to have moved on by the time you read this)

- Elena Tikhomirova at http://e-learningcenter.ru

I hope these sources help you better understand the changing nature of learning in the digital world.

UNDERSTANDING E-LEARNING

A good recent contribution to the e-learning debate is Shank, P (ed), *The Online Learning Idea Book: 95 proven ways to enhance technology-based and blended learning* (Pfeiffer, San Francisco, 2007), which collects its ideas under the following headings: supporting learners and learning, making collaboration work, making discussions work, self-directed and asynchronous activities, synchronous activities, self-check activities and assessments, the design and development process, navigation and usability, creative design and creative media.

The best collection of shorter writings I have encountered is a large volume edited by Allison Rossett that has stood the test of time quite well: Rossett, A, *The ASTD e-Learning Handbook: Best practices, strategies and case studies for an emerging field* (McGraw-Hill, New York, 2002). Allison's opening essay, 'Waking in the Night and Thinking about E-learning', will strike a chord with many learning and development professionals, and while the rest of the contributions vary in quality and usefulness, they amount to an impressive compendium. Here's a nice quotation from Allison's opening essay:

E-learning allows learning and performance professionals to do things we have always wanted to do: to deliver everywhere; to empower individuals; to coach; to collect and distribute best practices; to increase dialogue; to bust through the classroom walls; to increase community; and to know who is learning, referring to source materials, and contributing.

And Allison describes her 'big tent' view of e-learning in an interview at http://www.learningcircuits.org/2005/may2005/rossett.htm.

But if you only ever consult one website about e-learning, I would recommend that it should be http://www.e-learningguru.com. This is a portal run by the US learning professional and e-learning commentator Kevin Kruse, a vast repository of articles and resources for e-learning, and a gateway to other sources of information. But the best thing about it is the contrarian perspective of its editor; while other sites gleefully embrace all the latest fads, Kruse constantly questions them, sometimes adopts positions against the trends and always offers alternative views. A good, simple example of the excellent content of the E-learning Guru site is Kruse's short article 'Tricks, Traps and Other E-learning Vendor Shenanigans' at http://www.e-learningguru.com/articles/art6_5.htm, which I referenced in Chapter 4. Unfortunately, at the time of writing Kruse has moved away from e-learning and the Guru site has not been updated for some time, but it remains an invaluable archive.

An alternative portal, based in the United Kingdom, is the Learning Light E-learning Centre, which may be found at http://www.e-learning-centre.co.uk. The United Kingdom also has two industry associations, the E-learning Network in England and the eLearning Alliance in Scotland, both of which offer some public information at their websites. Around the world there are other similar associations in countries and regions on every continent (except, I think, Antarctica). Where they exist, these bodies can provide a very effective focus for bringing together different communities with a shared interest in e-learning, including not just corporate learning and development professionals and e-learning vendors, but academics from schools through to universities, researchers and representatives of professional associations and industry bodies, writers, consultants, designers, technologists and many others.

The American Society for Training and Development's 'source for e-learning' is http://www.learningcircuits.org, with both public parts and further resources exclusively for subscribing members.

In the United Kingdom the professional body for HR and learning and development managers is the 130,000-member-strong Chartered Institute of Personnel and Development, whose website is http://www.cipd.co.uk. The CIPD conducts an annual survey of learning and development trends, and e-learning is one the key areas of its inquiry. Thus, the CIPD can track developments in the field since its surveys started (in 2002), and summaries of each report are available on its website.

Arguably, the two leading e-learning consultants in the United States, if not the world, are Elliott Masie and Brandon Hall. Their respective sites are http://www.masieweb.com and http://www.brandon-hall.com. Masie tends to focus on ways of popularizing e-learning, such as through conferences and other events (not just in the United States), while Hall tends to focus on research. There are broader-based ICT research companies such as Gartner and International Data Corporation (IDC) that also produce research reports on e-learning, but Brandon Hall is more focused.

There are many more esoteric texts in the sphere of e-learning. Gilly Salmon's _E-moderating: The key to teaching and learning online_ (RoutledgeFalmer, Abingdon, 2004) is arguably one of the most valuable, and you can find a great deal of thinking on sub-topics such as 'e-tivities', 'e-mentoring' and e-portfolios. A good example of the last would be _The Educational Potential of E-portfolios: Supporting personal development and reflective learning (connecting with e-learning)_ by Lorraine Stefani, Robin Mason and Chris Pegler (Routledge, Abingdon, 2007).

E-portfolios are a particular interest of the European Institute for E-Learning (EIfEL), whose website is http://www.eife-l.org. Led by Serge Ravet, this organization has been very influential throughout Europe and beyond. This is its view of the importance of the e-portfolio: 'The worldwide emergence of the ePortfolio is transforming our current views on learning technologies. For the first time in the relatively short history of learning technologies we are seeing the rise of a new generation of tools dedicated to valuing and celebrating the achievements of the individual.'

The concepts of the three component parts of e-learning, and the five models of e-learning, are new, and in the present form at least are unique to this book. Echoes of them will be found elsewhere, including in some of my previous writing (see below), although discussion of related concepts may be found in many places. An interesting example is the October 2007 report 'Realising Value from On-line Learning in Management Development' by Professor William Scott-Jackson, Terry Edney and Ceri Rushent, published in the United Kingdom by the Chartered Management Institute in association with the Centre for Applied Human Resource Research at Oxford Brookes University and available for download at http://www.managers.org.uk/research reports.

These sources should lead you to an abundance of information to help you better understand e-learning.

ADVOCACY OF E-LEARNING

The concept of learner-centred learning is not new: I first came across it in the 1980s, and it probably pre-dates that period by some time. But the best recent restatement of the theory is in Martyn Sloman's *Training in the Age of the Learner* (CIPD, London, 2003), which specifically claims e-learning as the means to finally realize the vision. More recently, Sloman has added another work on this theme: Sloman, M, *The Changing World of the Trainer: Emerging good practice* (Butterworth-Heinemann, Oxford, 2007). Sloman successfully argues that in the new economy of the 21st century, service led, knowledge driven and equipped with e-learning resources, it is finally self-evident that learners should be at the centre of the process of learning.

On learning culture and learning organizations, the best place to start is Peter Senge's *The Fifth Discipline: The art and practice of the learning organization* (Random House, London, 1990), the book that really consolidated organizational learning theory.

The experiential learning cycle I cited is from David Kolb's *Experiential Learning: Experience as the source of learning and development* (Prentice Hall, Upper Saddle River, NJ, 1984). The subsequent work on learner style preferences by Peter Honey and Alan Mumford, also cited in Chapter 2, is in their *Manual of Learning Styles* (Honey, Maidenhead, 1992). The alternative learning styles theory I cited derives from Colin Rose's *Accelerated Learning* (Accelerated Learning Systems, Aylesbury, 1985).

In the spirit of experiential learning, there is a convenient collection of ideas in Watkins, R, *75 E-learning Activities: Making online learning interactive* (Pfeiffer, San Francisco, 2005), which also features a handy CD ROM.

Many of the texts referenced for Chapter 1 offer arguments and resources for advocacy of e-learning.

There is a wiki about the UC Davis Virtual Hallucination Clinic cited by Allison Rossett at http://slhealthy.wetpaint.com/page/Virtual+Hallucinations+(UC+DAVIS)?t=anon, and information about Martyn Sloman's choice of Hilton University at http://www.hilton-university.com.

The origins of my Impact Matrix lie in some CIPD research that Martyn Sloman described to me around 2004. Neither Martyn nor I have been able to find any published reference to this grid, and as I have since developed the idea further, I now claim it as my own. I subsequently borrowed some of the well-known symbolism of the Boston Consulting Group (BCG)'s Growth Share Matrix; more information about BCG can be found at its website, http://www.bcg.com, or by web searches for the Growth Share Matrix.

Hopefully, some of the sources cited in this section can help you make your case for e-learning.

E-LEARNING STRATEGY: DEVELOPMENT

We started our discussion on strategy with words of wisdom from Michael Porter. Porter has written many books, but his seminal works are *Competitive Strategy* (Free Press, New York, 1980) and *Competitive Advantage* (Free Press, New York, 1985). Anyone looking for more strategy gurus could do a lot worse than reading the work of Gary Hamel, notably *Competing for the Future* (Harvard Business School Press, Boston, 1996) (co-authored with C K Prahalad). This was the work that introduced the concept of core competence, which we used for our classification of e-learning suppliers in Chapter 4.

John Kay is my favourite writer on business strategy, and the quotations in Chapter 3 come from his *Foundations of Corporate Success* (Oxford University Press, Oxford, 1993). A more digestible, more recent and much more fun collection of his writing on the same theme may be found in *The Hare and the Tortoise* (Erasmus, London, 2006). Kay writes a pithy column in the *Financial Times* once a fortnight, which may also be accessed online at http://www.ft.com.

When it comes to applying strategy to specific business functions or more specialized areas, in the field of learning and development I found John Walton's *Strategic Human Resource Development* (FT Prentice Hall, Harlow, 1999) especially useful, although it was written just before e-learning took off and therefore omits to mention it at all.

Six years ago, Don Morrison wrote a very good book, *E-learning Strategies* (Wiley, London, 2003), which in some ways is the precursor to this volume, although I do not think he shares my views on standards or vendors (and perhaps one or two other things). I first heard of Don when, at a conference, he argued that we would know when the e-learning industry was established because industry jokes would start to appear. He offered his own contribution to start us off:

'What do you get if you cross an e-learning consultant with the Mafia?'
'Someone who makes you an offer you can't understand.'

Like all good jokes, it touched a nerve. In a similar vein, here's my offering:

'How many e-learning vendor staff does it take to change a light bulb?'
'I don't know... one to execute the task, one to adapt for the web, one to provide the hosting, one to provide the annual software support and maintenance contract, one to explain the e-learning standards specification, one project manager, one to manage the account... how big a budget do you have?'

Of course, I don't think there really is an 'e-learning industry' as such. A marketplace where software developers meet learning and development professionals, yes; and perhaps some niche vendors; but that's all.

Morrison's book remained one of only two e-learning books written from a strategic perspective that I've ever heard of – until now. I have cited a number of Morrison's useful contributions, including his 10-step procedure for selecting suppliers, in chapter 9 of his *E-learning Strategies* – perhaps a little deliberate and didactic for some tastes, but useful at least as a checklist of what to cover.

The other book with the same plural notion of e-learning strategies as Morrison's is Kahn, B, *Managing E-learning Strategies: Design, delivery, implementation and evaluation* (Idea Group Publishing, Hershey, 2005). Badrul Khan's book has a more academic orientation than Morrison's, and for me doesn't work as well in its exploration of strategy, but one unusual and distinguishing aspect of the book is that it features an entire chapter on ethical issues in e-learning, which may merit further exploration.

The most recent and most authoritative work on project management specifically for e-learning is Lynch, M M and Roecker, J, *Project Managing E-learning: A handbook for successful design, delivery and management* (Routledge, New York, 2007). Straddling the worlds of business and academia, but perhaps with more of an emphasis on the latter, it is based on a generic planning model not discussed in this book, 'IPECC', which stands for Initiate, Plan, Execute, Control and Close.

The quality assurance model in Chapter 3 is derived from similar work developed in 2000 by a UK National Health Service (NHS) organization, the former National Board for Nursing, Midwifery and Health Visiting for Scotland, now part of NHS Education for Scotland. See www.qacpd.org.uk.

The references in this section should offer a more complete view of the overall subject of business strategy, and a better understanding of its application to e-learning.

E-LEARNING STRATEGY: SUPPLIERS AND RESOURCES

There is a dearth of literature about e-learning suppliers, other than their own websites. And there is very little about e-learning technologies that is not written to promote particular products. That is one of the reasons why Chapter 4 is the longest in this book: the need to provide guidance on these issues. I find it rather telling that there is such a lack of effort by techies to explain themselves to the wider world.

The European Institute for E-Learning publishes a report on e-learning platforms and tools that assesses their relative merits, but that presupposes you are interested in buying one of these products in the first place.

Of course, product lines can be researched on the web, with vendors often offering extensive information and free demos of their products, as long as you are wary of their natural bias. There are also sites that review comparable products, and lots of information about open-source software.

As an illustration, there are several open-source virtual learning environments that can be examined online. The only one I have used is Moodle (http://moodle.org), which seems to be the most popular, but there are several others:

Atutor (http://www.atutor.ca),
Claroline (http://www.claroline.net/worldwide.htm),
Dokeos (http://www.dokeos.com),
Efrontlearning (http://www.efrontlearning.net),
Kewl (http://kngforge.uwc.ac.za),
Campus Source (http://www.campussource.de),
OLAT (http://www.olat.org)
and Sakai (http://www.sakaiproject.org).

A measure of Moodle's popularity is that there is now at least one book specifically about e-learning development for it: Rice, W, *Moodle E-learning Course Development* (Packt Publishing, Birmingham, 2006).

An open-source authoring tool is eXe, and information about it may be found at http://www.kineo.com, but one immediate drawback is that it must be used in conjunction with the Firefox web browser.

There is a link to a review of authoring tools at http://store.bersinassociates.com/authtools.html, and links to further reviews of e-learning tools and systems at http://www.keele.ac.uk/depts/aa/landt/lt/docs/vlereviews.htm.

The e-learning value chain model referenced in the e-learning industry section was published in an economic report: Fee, K, *eLearning in Scotland* (eLearning Alliance, Glasgow, 2002).

The primary source for SCORM is http://www.adlnet.gov/scorm, which offers the definition I have quoted, but of course this is not a dispassionate source, as ADL owns SCORM. Indeed, it is difficult to find any truly objective commentary on SCORM; web searches throw up innumerable software consultants whose business is implementing SCORM, but no critics. Fiona Leteny has contributed an admirably light and accessible series of articles to *e.learning age* magazine (see http://www.elearningage.co.uk), spanning many months, but even these take it for granted that SCORM is A

Good Thing. Find out what you can, and make up your own mind. Leteny has also written a useful introductory article, a 'Beginners' Guide to e-Learning Standards', at http://www.towardsmaturity.org, a resource promoted by e-skills UK.

The distinction between conformance and compliance, which is not universally shared but which I nevertheless consider helpful, comes from CETIS, the Centre for Educational Technology and Interoperability Standards. See http://assessment.cetis.ac.uk for further information. CETIS is an initiative of the Joint Information Systems Committee for higher education in the United Kingdom.

A useful treatment of the use of collaborative tools for learning is Richardson, W, *Blogs, Wikis, Podcasts, and Other Powerful Web Tools for Classrooms* (Corwin Press, Thousand Oaks, CA, 2006), although its focus is schools in the United States. The source of my user stats for Wikipedia is an article in the *Observer* magazine, published in the United Kingdom, 'For Your Information', by Tim Adams, 1 July 2007.

I hope these sources help you better understand the technology issues associated with e-learning, including getting to grips with the jargon, making your mind up about standards and specifications, and getting under the fingernails of e-learning vendors.

E-LEARNING STRATEGY: LEARNING DESIGN ISSUES

There have been a number of books that have tried to provide specialist advice in the field of e-learning design. Some of them betray a serious lack of understanding of what is involved in learning. A useful rule of thumb is to steer clear of any that talk of 'instructional design', as they are not likely to be learner centred (although that would mean dismissing most of the literature from the United States). But recently I have been impressed by Chapnick, S and Meloy, J, *Renaissance eLearning: Creating Dramatic and Unconventional Learning Experiences* (Pfeiffer, San Francisco, 2005), and I quoted a series of key points from this work in Chapter 5. Another impressive offering is Allen, M, *Michael Allen's Guide to E-learning: Building interactive, fun and effective learning programs for any company* (John Wiley & Sons, Hoboken, NJ, 2003). What both books have in common includes a learner-centred approach, a willingness to learn from other design contexts, a creative approach and an interest in making the learning enjoyable for the learners.

William Horton's *E-learning by Design* (Pfeiffer, San Francisco, 2006) uses the flawed 'instructional design' perspective but is a decent guide to utilizing the various tools and techniques available, from the standpoint of 'here's a list of what you can do and how you should use each feature'. An interesting comparison is Michael Allen's more recent *Designing Successful E-learning: Forget what you know about instructional design and do something interesting* (Pfeiffer, San Francisco, 2007), which opens with a useful series of high-profile case studies.

Two of the most stimulating contributions of recent years have been by Marc Prensky on games and Clark Aldrich on simulations. These two authors are widely acknowledged as the leading authorities in their respective specialist areas. Their works that provide the best overviews are Prensky, M, *Digital Game-based Learning* (McGraw-Hill, New York, 2004; first edition published 2001), and Aldrich, C, *Learning by Doing: A comprehensive guide to simulations, computer games, and pedagogy in e-learning and other educational experiences* (Pfeiffer, San Francisco, 2005). More recently, they have collaborated on an invaluable compendium of writings bringing together these concepts under the umbrella of experiential learning: Gibson, D, Aldrich, C and Prensky, M (eds), *Games and Simulations in Online Learning: Research and development frameworks* (Information Science Publishing, Hershey, PA, 2007).

The classic work on communities of practice is Wenger, E, *Communities of Practice: Learning, meaning, and identity* (Learning in Doing: Social, Cognitive and Computational Perspectives, Cambridge University Press, Cambridge, 1998 – and reprinted eight times since). And there is a substantial resource for self-managed learning at Etienne Wenger's website, http://www.ewenger.com. Wenger has much to teach us about the design of learning experiences.

There is very little literature on designing live e-learning. The best I can find is Barclay, K *et al*, *The Live E-learning Cookbook: Recipes for success* (iUniverse.com, Bloomington, IN, 2003).

If there is little on live e-learning, there is a desert when it comes to books on electronic performance support systems, with the most recent titles dating from the mid-1990s, before e-learning took off, and therefore being of very limited value. If curious, you could try something like Brown, L A, *Designing and Developing Electronic Performance Support Systems* (Butterworth-Heinemann, Newton, MA, 1996).

I hope these references encourage you to get involved in helping build a new theory of e-learning design.

E-LEARNING STRATEGY: MEASUREMENT AND RESULTS

There have been several editions of the key text for the first approach cited in Chapter 6, the latest being Kirkpatrick, D L, *Evaluating Training Programs: The four levels* (Berrett-Koehler, San Francisco, 1996). Kirkpatrick has also made countless further written contributions on this theme, dating back to the 1950s.

There is much to find on return on investment (ROI) in general in books and journals and on the web. The ROI Institute (http://www.roi-institute.net) describes itself as 'the leading resource on research, training, and networking for practitioners of the Phillips ROI Methodology'. Looking at ROI specifically for learning and development, there are works such as Kearns, P, *Evaluating the ROI from Learning: How to develop value-based training* (CIPD, London, 2005). Even more specifically, for ROI for e-learning there is a collection of white papers, articles, case studies and calculators at http://www.e-learningguru.com/knowledge_roi.htm.

The Kevin Kruse quotation about the limitations of ROI comes from his article 'Enough already! Getting off the ROI bandwagon' at http://www.e-learningguru.com/articles/art5_8.htm. Kevin's CASE acronym, also cited in Chapter 6, comes from the same article.

Ulrich, D and Brockbank, W, *The HR Value Proposition* (Harvard Business School Press, Boston, 2005) provides the starting point for our discussion of return on expectation (ROE). CIPD research on ROE has been summarized online at the CIPD website since late 2007, and the same body also published an important new book around the same time, based on the research results: Anderson, V, *The Value of Learning: From return on investment to return on expectation* (CIPD, London, 2007).

As previously noted, there is plenty of literature on Six Sigma, such as Pyzdek, T, *The Six Sigma Handbook, Revised and Expanded: A complete guide for greenbelts, blackbelts and managers at all levels* (McGraw-Hill, New York, 2003), or the website http://www.isixsigma.com, which includes a useful dictionary and glossary. Applying Six Sigma specifically to learning, and to e-learning, is a relatively new idea first developed in a book by Islam, K A, *Developing and Measuring Training the 6 Sigma Way: A business approach to training and development* (Pfeiffer, San Francisco, 2006). And there is plenty more to be found on Six Sigma in general.

The definition of intellectual capital quoted in Chapter 6 is from 'Profiting from Intellectual Capital', an article by Patrick H Sullivan in the *Journal of Knowledge Management*, volume 3, number 2.

Thomas Stewart's *Intellectual Capital: The new wealth of organizations* (Doubleday, New York, 1997) is one of the best books I have ever read. In this book, and its preceding articles in *Fortune* magazine, Stewart practically invented the discipline of knowledge management. As an insight into the existence of value beyond the balance sheet, it remains unsurpassed. In the appendix to his book, Stewart offers a number of 'tools for measuring and managing intellectual capital', which provide a good starting point for going on to explore the kind of value we can show beyond 'book value'. But please take the time to read everything Stewart writes before the appendix!

The Learning Light e-Learning Centre has a large number of articles exploring the issue of evaluating the effectiveness of e-learning at http://www.e-learningcentre.co.uk/eclipse/Resources/effective.htm.

I trust these references will provide you with further study, and a deeper insight, into issues of e-learning evaluation.

E-LEARNING IN THE FUTURE

Steven Pinker's *How the Mind Works* (Penguin, London, 1997) does not just provide a pithy saying ridiculing poor-quality predictions of the future but reinforces the argument against vendors in Chapter 4. If the mind really is such a complicated mechanism, and we really are so far from fully understanding how it – and, by implication, learning – works, then how much more foolhardy are the claims of e-learning vendors to understand learning and to offer solutions? Pinker's work generally, and not just the book quoted, provides a fascinating background to this intriguing topic.

Linden Lab's Second Life is one of the biggest phenomena in digital technology ever. If you think that is hype, take a look at http://secondlife.com and consider joining and developing a second life of your own. Or look at the financial information available at http://secondlife.reuters.com, or read the official blog at http://blog.secondlife.com. Or explore the commentary on it all over the web – but bear in mind that you can only learn so much from outside.

The Learning Light e-Learning Centre has a large number of articles exploring the issue of learning and the future of learning at http://www.e-learningcentre.co.uk/eclipse/Resources/learning.htm.

Please use these references to look beyond the epilogue of this book into the world of e-learning in the future.

BLOGS

This is a short selection of e-learning blogs I have visited from time to time. This list does not imply any endorsement, but they are all interesting in their own way, and collectively they are intended to give an overall flavour of what is out there.

- Bryan Chapman at http://brandon-hall.com/bryanchapman
- Donald Clark at http://donaldclarkplanb.blogspot.com
- Jay Cross at http://informl.com
- Michelle Gallen at http://www.liquidelearning.com
- Paul Justice at http://www.innerpsyche.blogspot.com
- Tony Karrer at http://elearningtech.blogspot.com
- Elliott Masie at http://trends.masie.com
- Nigel Paine at http://www.nigelpaine.com/blog
- Clive Shepherd at http://clive-shepherd.blogspot.com
- Jenna Sweeney at http://www.cramersweeney.com/cs_id/training-blog
- Elena Tikhomirova at http://www.elearningtime.blogspot.com (in Russian)
- David Wilson (and colleagues) at http://elearnity.blogspot.com

There are also many discussion forums and subscription-based online communities for people interested or involved in e-learning. Please make the effort not only to read the blogs, or lurk in these communities, but also to contribute, make comments and get involved. Doing so will help you much more with your self-development.

MY EARLIER WRITING

There are sections on e-learning and related ideas such as virtual learning centres in my *Guide to Management Development Techniques* (Kogan Page, London, 2001). I must admit that my thinking about e-learning reflected in that book (written between 2000 and 2001) was rather limited. Since 2002, most of my writing has been on e-learning, including the 2002 economic report *E-learning in Scotland* and the e-learning chapter in the

CIPD's *Learning and Development* manual, a subscription publication issued from 2007 to 2008. I have also written a number of e-learning articles for various UK journals. My first article 'E-learning Strategy' appeared at www.learnforever.co.uk in January 2007, and my second, 'Paint the Bigger Picture', available at the same website, originally appeared in the June 2007 edition of *e.learning age* magazine.

I should like to close with the quotation I use for the masthead of my website, and for my blog. It's a good quote, albeit perhaps apocryphal. I haven't been able to confirm an original source, and some people attribute it to Gandhi, while others think it was Einstein. Whoever it was, the sentiment is consistent with the message of this chapter: 'Live like you are going to die tomorrow, learn like you are going to live for ever.'

This review of references, annotated bibliography and guide to sources for your further learning about e-learning brings the main body of this book to an end. But the ongoing development of e-learning, and your personal development related to it, still has a long way to go. In the epilogue we shall draw some conclusions and look to the future.

SUMMARY OF KEY POINTS

1. Learning and development professionals, and everyone interested in e-learning, need to learn more about e-learning and commit themselves to personal development with a view to implementing e-learning strategies and transforming e-learning for the future.

That's all.

Epilogue:
E-learning in the future

SOME CONCLUSIONS

E-learning is here to stay. Some organizations continue to ignore it, but they are getting fewer and fewer in number, and once the digital natives take over, there will be none. Learning and development professionals need to recognize the reality of learning in the digital age and ensure that their organizations are responsive to their people's needs.

E-learning can hardly claim to have been a great success so far; for every positive implementation there is a horror story, and many people retain a resistance to e-learning based on these experiences. If e-learning were just a passing fad, it would have passed away by now, murdered many times over by the mortal weight of failures. But its champions persevere despite the imbalance of the current evidence, because we look at the bigger picture and we know it is the way ahead.

Among the reasons for e-learning's failures so far are the mystification of techie jargon that serves to exclude many of those who need to be included; confusion about e-learning standards and specifications; lack of understanding of what is involved in learning, especially on the part of would-be e-learning vendors; vendors failing to get to grips with what the market needs; and learning and development professionals being unsure how to proceed. And more; all of which we need to unpick.

The key to implementing successful e-learning is to develop an e-learning strategy that is right for your organization and constantly review what you do against that strategy. This book offers guidance on how to do that. In summary: you need to have a complete understanding of e-learning and be clear in your advocacy of it; you need to develop an e-learning strategy with a strong vision derived from your organization's inherent capabilities and aligned with your business and learning and development strategies; you need to recognize the technological resources at your disposal and marshal them to maximum effect; you need to design your e-learning initiatives in line with your strategy; and you need to measure and evaluate your e-learning in such a way as to achieve the best results for your organization.

These are the headlines. Behind them are stories too numerous to tell, hopefully summarized in the 50 key points I have appended to the end of the chapters, which are collated into a full list at the end of the book. We need to retain a positive outlook about e-learning's potential, while learning from the serious mistakes made so far.

Part of our new awareness must be to look ahead and consider how e-learning may change; if we can anticipate change, we can be prepared to adapt to it.

LOOKING TO THE FUTURE

In this book I have tried to summarize what has gone wrong with e-learning over the past decade, where e-learning is now, and where it should be. Human beings retain their desire to learn and achieve personal growth. Technology continues to develop and improve, and while some of us are more disadvantaged than others in terms of what we can access, generally speaking there is no technological constraint to hold us back, and there is no major financial obstacle to e-learning being transformed in the kind of way I believe it should be. The only limitation is our will to make it happen.

We need to learn from the lessons of the past, but we also need to look to the future. In the Industrial Age the focus of training was on skill development; in the Digital Age the emphasis for learning and development has shifted to knowledge and its application. There remain construction and extractive operations, engineering and manufacturing companies, and others, where the advancement of manipulative skills is still a big priority, but much more of modern learning focuses on knowledge and applied knowledge. It is against this background that we should consider the criticism of e-learning that it is better for knowledge-based, rather than skill-based, learning. The inescapable conclusion is that e-learning is better fitted to the learning needs of the 21st century.

The barriers to e-learning, notwithstanding the mistakes that have been made in implementing it, seem to be largely about the reluctance of older learners to become digital immigrants. As the population of digital natives grows, it is inevitable that e-learning will come into its own. One conclusion learning and development managers should draw is that it is imperative that they find ways to implement successful e-learning.

But the news is not all good. According to the CIPD's 2008 learning and development survey for the United Kingdom, more than half of responding organizations now use e-learning, but only 7 per cent rank it in their top three most effective training practices. This suggests something of a crisis of confidence in e-learning, in the United Kingdom at least. Addressing this report, Martyn Sloman reiterated his belief that e-learning is here to stay, but that learning and development professionals need to take greater ownership of it to help embed it more effectively in organizations. 'Far too much of it', he has said, 'is driven by the IT department and not HR. Organizations are chucking e-learning out there at unsupported learners. It needs to be specifically tailored to their use.'

I am optimistic about the future of e-learning, but learning and development professionals will have to take a lead in transforming the way we utilize digital technology to take our organizations forward. We have seen in this book that there is a lot of bad practice to overcome, and we shall need to work to ensure that more people start to see e-learning as more effective.

Looking ahead to try to foresee what may happen in the future is fraught with difficulty.

John Kenneth Galbraith said, 'There are those who don't know, and there are those who don't know they don't know.' At the moment, there seem to me to be many people involved in e-learning who do not realize that there are problems, and until they achieve this insight, they remain blind to what they do not know. Many need to move from unconscious incompetence to conscious incompetence before they can begin to attain conscious competence and thence strive for unconscious competence, or excellence, or at least something more.

THE EXACT SCIENCE OF HINDSIGHT

In 2007 I wrote a chapter on e-learning for a general learning and development manual, in which I divided my predictions for the future into the short term (up to 5 years), the medium term (5 to 10 years) and the longer term (10 years and beyond). There is some merit in this subdivision (and none of my chickens has come home to roost yet), but it is extremely difficult to predict with any accuracy not just what may happen but when things are going to happen. Even in instances where we have a good idea that an invention is imminent, or participation in something is going to reach a point where it achieves a critical mass, predicting a specific time-frame can be little more than guesswork. But this does not mean that the entire exercise is futile.

Steven Pinker, in his book *How the Mind Works*, talks about 'the emotional debate over What Computers Will-Soon/Won't-Ever Do' and makes some observations about the futility of longer-range forecasting. Citing, among other examples, Lord Kelvin's late-19th-century assessment that 'heavier-than-air flying machines are impossible', he concludes that 'the one prediction coming out of futurology that is undoubtedly correct is that in the future today's futurologists will look silly'. Nevertheless, we braver souls persist, unafraid of the mocking of future generations.

Against that background, predicting what is going to happen in the immediate future can be relatively straightforward. In any growing market we can predict more of the same, plus incremental improvements. We can expect more e-learning to take place, more platforms and tools to be tried out, more learning and development professionals to become skilled in the use of ICT applications for learning, and organizations and employees to become more receptive to e-learning. We can expect to make more progress and we can expect to hear more success stories.

One has learned to be wary of the wilder predictions, and nobody is likely to make the sort of claims that were being made for e-learning as recently as seven or eight years ago. Some thought that e-learning would quickly grow from less than 10 per cent of an organization's training delivery (where it was) to more than 50 per cent (where it has not yet reached), and were forced to revise their time estimates when that did not happen.

John Chambers of Cisco Systems notoriously claimed, in 2000, 'The next big killer application on the internet is going to be education. Education over the internet is going to be so big it is going to make e-mail usage look like a rounding error.'

Three or four years on, as e-mail usage continued to make e-learning usage 'look like a rounding error', forecasters had gone quiet on e-learning. At least the era of overselling was over.

Analysts in recent years have been keen to predict 'new waves' of e-learning – e-learning 2.0 is just one example – but this is based more on the weaknesses and failures of e-learning to date (and thence the need for new waves) than on any credible evidence of their occurring. According to early predictions like Chambers', e-learning should have transformed the world of work by now, but in the main it hasn't. Digital technology is changing our lives, but e-learning is not changing apace.

As an interesting example, online social networking while at work, such as accessing sites like Facebook in the office, has been irritating business commentators, managers and HR professionals alike. There has been alarm at the threat it poses to productivity and retaining employees' focus on work. But the fears are largely groundless. By the time you read this, the scaremongers may have moved on to something else, but in any event, I doubt that the concerns about social networking will last. Like many issues with digital technology (cf the discussion on e-assessment in Chapter 4), what has happened is that something that has always been a problem has been brought to the surface because it is now more visible, recordable and traceable. Employees have always wasted time in casual conversation and pursuit of personal interests and other distractions at work; in most instances it was not a serious problem when it was face to face or over the phone, so why should it suddenly become one online?

I suspect what we are seeing with social networking is just the beginning, and people will find more new ways to interact with a much wider community of contacts, using digital technology. It will become a much bigger issue, to the extent that recent concerns will seem laughable, rather like old concerns that giving employees desktop PCs would lead to their spending all day playing with the technology. The distinctions between work time and personal time will become blurred (learning has always taken place during both, anyway), and if this leads employers to focus more on results rather than on time-serving, then that should be a good thing. If we could encourage people to use this technology to spend more time learning, most of us would be delighted.

WHAT WE CAN DO

Gradually we are reaching a better understanding of what e-learning is and what it can help achieve. This is a start. It is therefore likely that in the immediate future we will reach a shared understanding of this, consequently implement e-learning more effectively, and consequently arrive at a more accurate assessment of its worth. I believe e-learning vendors will start to recognize the errors that have compounded their work to date, and limited their growth. Many of them will break with the bad habits of the past and become more responsive to their clients, while the ones that don't will probably go out of business. I hope e-learning vendors will read this book and learn from their, or their competitors', mistakes.

I also believe learning and development professionals will start to understand and utilize e-learning better. And, key to that, we will all start to take a more strategic approach to implementing successful e-learning.

We need to start from the indisputable assumption that digital technology is with us, it is now and will always be an inherent part of how we learn, and new generations of learners will have increasing expectations about digital technology serving their learning needs. Therefore, we need to find new ways of implementing e-learning that actually address these needs. Learning and development professionals and e-learning vendors can make common cause in bringing this about; senior managers with the right vision can point them in this direction; all of us can bring pressure to bear to make this happen.

And we can extend the debate, and learn from the visions others have of what is coming in the future.

Virtual Round Table: Part 4

I asked our international experts to look ahead, to think about how e-learning will change in the future and to speculate as to what it could look like in 10 years' time.

Martyn Sloman foresees 'a gradual process of more and more people using e-learning, because more people will be using a computer at work, and we're getting better at making e-learning relevant'. And the same sense of incremental change appears in others' thinking.

Allison Rossett simply predicts 'more Sims, more games, more on-demand assets. More blended learning'.

Nigel Paine expects 'more complexity, and e-learning more tailored to the needs and proclivities of individual learners. And more granular, so that material can be configured on the fly to meet the needs of an individual'.

Marius Meyer anticipates 'quicker and faster technology, perhaps elements of it on cell phones and other forms of mobile technology. A greater emphasis on work–life balance and a real trend towards a virtual office will facilitate the proper implementation of e-learning. Although e-learning has huge benefits, a more blended approach to learning will probably be used in future. More emphasis will be placed on measuring the impact of e-learning, and greater cooperation between the learning and ICT functions will be needed'.

Elena Tikhomirova believes that 'Web 2.0 technologies give us new possibilities of interactions. Today's internet has changed from reading to authoring. The next big thing in e-learning will be learners having more freedom and taking a bigger part in content generation. E-learning will move from just learning to knowledge sharing and knowledge management. I believe that e-learning will have bigger success when associated as the most powerful tool for knowledge management.'

Serge Ravet has a more revolutionary vision of 'the emergence of "digital identity"; learners will develop their own digital assets and will become more knowledge producers rather than consumers. There will be personal learning environments along-side organizational learning environments (learning manage-ment systems are really training management systems, and are not designed for SMEs [small and medium-sized enterprises]). What we really need is a series of communities, not a big corpo-rate system, especially for professional development'.

In the longer term, Marius sees some major issues: 'The biggest challenge is to help traditional classroom-based trainers and learn-ers to see the benefit of e-learning. Many people in Africa don't have access to technology, so the digital divide exacerbates the problem. As more companies globalize, e-learning will be one of the most important learning tools to distribute learning across the globe irrespective of the different time zones. Ultimately, e-learn-ing requires a better integration between the different phases of the learning process, thereby ensuring greater alignment between needs analysis, design, learning facilitation and evaluation.'

Elena adds, 'E-learning should be adaptive. When entering an e-learning course or programme, the learner will take a pre-test and according to its results the content and the sequence of learn-ing objects should be generated to achieve maximum fulfilment of individual learning needs. In the era of information overload, people will start to select more carefully what they learn in order to avoid unnecessary information.'

Nigel looks forward to '3D learning'. This will mean 'spaces you walk into and grab resources, share and learn with others in that space and explore what is available rather than what is pre-sented to you as a learner'. His enthusiasm boils over: 'The most exciting time is to come.'

Serge reckons, 'The term "e-learning" will disappear (for digital natives, it will be unnecessary). Technology will simply be another enabler for all learning. It will be embedded and will be virtually invisible.'

Martyn Sloman has the final word, emphasizing that, ultimately, e-learning is more about people than about technology. 'There won't be any major change occasioned by new turnkey technology, and people will not learn in significantly different ways because human beings have not changed in any fundamental way.'

SOME PREDICTIONS

New technology often breaks though suddenly and unexpectedly. It is conceivable that something unheard of today could be the Next Big Thing within a year and could be in widespread use within three. Or it could take a little longer. Or it could never happen at all. The technology to support affordable videophones in the home has existed for at least 20 years, while people have been separated from friends and family they rarely see because they live on other continents. Throughout the 1990s I expected a mass consumer boom in videophones almost every year. Yet videophones never took off, and have been superseded by web-based applications. So, unlike hindsight, this certainly is not an exact science. A broader look at what is happening and what is expected to happen with digital technology in general ought to yield some pointers for e-learning, but this approach has not been very helpful in the past. Nevertheless, we can make some educated guesses about this sort of thing. Here are four or five significant developments that I predict will unfold in the foreseeable future and help to transform e-learning.

Virtual reality is something that has not really taken off in e-learning the way it was predicted it would, some five years ago. The term refers to technology that allows the user to interact with a simulated environment (real or imaginary), and encounter and overcome the problems that arise. There are signs that it is taking off in the gaming industry, with developments beyond the purely audio-visual to include tactile information, and this could be useful for learning applications. The barrier to growth has been limitation of processing power, but this will be overcome soon, just as bandwidth problems were resolved. Thus, we may see virtual reality become a staple of e-learning in the medium term.

If you doubt the potential of virtual reality, think of applications as old as flight simulators for aeroplane pilots, then take a look at Second Life, an online world with a huge 'population' (real subscribers) and a thriving economy. At the time of writing, subscriptions to Second Life exceed the population of Greater London, and such is its growth that by the time you read this they may have exceeded the population of the metropolitan New York area.

Mobile learning must surely grow in scale of use and in complexity. The term itself has not really taken off, and nor should it, for we already have a plethora of superfluous jargon in the e-learning field. But the concept is sound. Some have remained dubious about the usefulness of handheld devices such as mobile phones and personal digital assistants (PDAs) for e-learning, but this scepticism was based on doubt about how much information can be displayed on a miniature screen – and e-learning is about more than what can be displayed. What mobile learning should harness above all is the power of handhelds as communication tools, and, as we have discussed, electronic performance support (EPS) may be one of the drivers of this growth. The ubiquity of wireless telecommunications networks should help drive this development.

As handhelds become more sophisticated, it seems likely that people will be using them to learn much more, and this break from the environment of the desktop or laptop PC may open up new ways of thinking about how technology can aid learning.

One possibility is that handhelds will become *wrist-mounted devices*. A few years ago I heard about the research and development functions of mobile phone companies investigating the potential of flexible polymers. Their work suggested that future mobile learning may be based on miniature computers worn wrapped around the underside of the left wrist (for right-handed people). This kind of device would replace the wristwatch, the mobile phone, the personal digital assistant (PDA) and entertainment devices such as the iPod. If that happens, its use for learning seems inevitable. However, it is now more than four years since I heard of this, and no product has hit the market. I suspect a stumbling block has been the increase in the use of phones as cameras. The wrist-mounted scenario would not suit taking either stills or video clips; try manipulating your wrist as you would have to for photography and you will see what I mean. I expect there will be a breakthrough in this field sooner or later: we have a clear need for a single portable device that will integrate all the bits and pieces we carry around, and it is just a question of sorting out the ergonomics.

Perhaps the biggest likely development we can predict with some confidence will be in *new interfaces*. How we use computers and work online will change, and the standard interfaces we use at the moment – the mouse and the keyboard – will become obsolete. Voice recognition and handwriting recognition software, and touch-sensitive screens, show the way ahead. How much longer will it be until, like Mr Spock in *Star Trek*, we simply talk to our computer and it talks back to us? And then there are the headsets and controls of virtual reality applications, which suggest other ways of working. As we adopt more natural ways of interacting with digital technologies, it is inevitable that they will become more pervasive in all aspects of our lives, not just learning. In the not-too-distant future, the devices we take for granted today may come to be regarded as little more than glorified typewriters. Even the desktop or laptop computer is under threat, as handheld devices can increasingly replicate the work of their bigger counterparts, and the long-term trend in electronics is always for devices to get smaller. The development of interactive television points to a new approach: homes are not likely to have separate television sets and computers for much longer. Similarly, we now have many domestic appliances controllable, even remotely, from microprocessors: refrigerators and microwave ovens can be instructed to chill, defrost or cook food, central heating can be switched on or off, and the most advanced 'smart homes' can now integrate many of these activities. More intuitive user interfaces are surely just around the corner.

Personal learning environments are the logical development of increased personalization in virtual learning environments (VLEs). The idea is that each individual learner will have his or her own web space linked to all the resources that that person requires, a kind of enhanced version of our third model of e-learning. In personal learning environments, learners will achieve the ultimate in blended learning, picking and choosing the elements that suit them and rejecting whatever they consider unsuitable. This vision is here already, and is perhaps held back from reality only by the vested interests of VLE vendors, who will need to position themselves to offer these more personalized solutions instead of their current products. Or they may just simply go out of business, their core products having become obsolete. Getting there from where we are now may be problematic; otherwise this development could occur much sooner.

BEYOND THE PREDICTABLE

It is, of course, possible that some of the developments described will happen faster or more slowly; the above predictions could happen within a year or two, or 5 years, or 10. Or they may not happen at all. As Pinker warned us, that is the nature of future-gazing: we are dealing with, among other things, the unexpected and the unpredictable. But given the rate of technological innovation and change we have seen in the past 10 years – how many of us had e-mail and web browsers 10 years ago? – we should not be cautious about the prospects for the next decade and beyond. As Gary Hamel and C K Prahalad put it, 'only those who can imagine and pre-emptively create the future will be around to enjoy it'.

If we explore the potential beyond new interfaces and personal learning environments, it may be that computer chips will be embedded in our brains, rendering obsolete our need for physical contact with external hardware of any kind. Only a generation ago, this sort of prediction would have been regarded as the wilder reaches of science fiction, but today we can see the possibilities. It is not inconceivable that this sort of technological application will be the norm within our lifetimes.

What will the world look like in 10 years' time or more? It is hard to imagine, and how we learn will be just one, relatively small, part of that world. But most of us will be here to witness it, and many of us will live much longer into the future. Katie, Devinder and Sam can expect to grow up in a world that appears to us dominated by digital technology but will in equal measure be instinctive and invisible to them. I look forward to the prospect of sharing it with them as long as possible, and I commit myself to the task of helping ensure that we can offer e-learning provision to fulfil their aspirations.

I hope you will join me in that task; you will find it rewarding. The potential for e-learning really is unlimited.

SUMMARY OF ALL THE KEY POINTS IN THIS BOOK

1. There are many misconceptions about e-learning, most notably a narrow view of what it is, derived from the limited scope of early e-learning implementations.

2. Our working definition of e-learning is that it is an approach to learning and development, a collection of learning methods using digital technologies, which enable, distribute and enhance learning.

3. E-learning has three distinct but complementary components: enabling technology, learning content and learning design.

4. E-learning is best understood as an approach to learning, not a method. It is an aggregation of a number of related methods. It is an approach that is undervalued, and promises greater potential for all aspects of learning for work.

5. We can identify five discrete models of e-learning: online courses, integrated online and offline learning ('blended learning'), self-managed e-learning, live e-learning and electronic performance support (EPS).

6. There are many different ways of blending online and offline learning, which we can recognize as the milestone, the sandwich, the knowledge and skill blend, and the blending of complementary resources – and probably many others.

7. Some superfluous jargon has emerged under the banners of e-learning 2.0 and learning 2.0 to try to express the potential of social networking for learning. But this jargon does not help most people understand e-learning any better.

8. E-learning can play a major role in making learning more learner centred, developing a learning culture, building a learning organization and empowering learners.

9. In the digital age it is impossible to ignore e-learning. Every organization will need to develop e-learning in response to employee and other stakeholder expectations.

10. E-learning has many benefits and various capabilities in different contexts. You need to work out what are the best benefits for your organization.

11. E-learning can offer something to suit every learning style preference, and may be the best option for some learning styles.

12. There are five criteria to consider when choosing an e-learning approach. In sequence, these are learning needs, learner style preferences, cost, time and value-add.

13. When advocating e-learning, you need to develop your influencing skills, master change management and aim to achieve a paradigm shift in your organization.

14. The Impact Matrix can help with the advocacy of e-learning in your organization, and in particular can demonstrate what sort of impact different kinds of e-learning will be likely to have.

15. E-learning can complement and support almost any organization development initiative.

16. There are three sets of circumstances when e-learning is not appropriate: where face-to-face involvement is necessary, when the learner actually has to be in the workplace and when the learner has to be exposed to something new. There are also some people who support e-learning for the wrong reasons.

17. Strategy is about linking your distinctive capabilities to achievable goals; it is more flexible than long-term planning, and forms a bridge between theory and practice.

18. Your e-learning strategy should be governed by the same principles as other strategies in your organization, and should be aligned to these other strategies, especially your learning and development strategy and your overall business strategy. You should start by looking at the broader context before narrowing your focus.

19. You need an explicit e-learning strategy statement because of the widespread confusion about e-learning.

20. Your e-learning strategy document should include clarification of what you mean by e-learning; aims and objectives; a framework for planning, and guidance to everyone involved; consideration of resources and partners; your models, approach and design principles; and how you will evaluate e-learning.

21. More detailed planning of e-learning initiatives should be based on the standard training and development cycle, and on the standard approach to planning you use in your organization.

22. You need to involve vendors, like all other stakeholders, in your strategy development, while being wary of their distractions and diversions.

23. You need to prepare to manage the quality of your e-learning via consideration of four dimensions: strategy setting, technology and resources, infrastructure, and results.

24. You need to constantly ask questions concerning what you are doing.

25. There is too much technological jargon associated with e-learning, and too many technology vendors use it to obfuscate e-learning.

26. The e-learning industry, in so far as such a thing exists, is very fragmented.

27. There are six categories of e-learning vendor: consultants; authors or developers; generic courseware vendors; virtual learning environment (VLE) providers; authoring tool providers; and providers of specialist software. Most vendors have core competence in just one of these categories.

28. The question of e-learning standards is a hot topic in e-learning but is largely irrelevant for most of us. We should understand that SCORM (Sharable Content Object Reference Model) is a collection of standards and specifications to enable interoperability, accessibility and reusability of web-based learning content, but we should not be enslaved by it.

29. A virtual learning environment is an enabling system for e-learning, which can be expensive but can be invaluable especially for large organizations that need scalable solutions. A VLE may include a learner management system (LMS), a learning content management system (LCMS) and a virtual classroom.

30. Authoring tools may be used by non-techies to create their own e-learning, often relatively quickly and easily, as in rapid content development, either independently or within a virtual learning environment.

31. There is a variety of additional specialist software available, notably e-assessment software, that may also be used independently or within a VLE.

32. Some of the more recently adopted software options, such as wikis, blogs, discussion forums and podcasts, increase the potential for learner participation, and for more interactive, and therefore more effective, e-learning.

33. Supplier relationships need to be managed in a positive way to make the most of them, and to add the maximum value.

34. Having a coherent and consistent approach to e-learning design is an essential part of having an e-learning strategy.

35. Design is one of the three component parts of e-learning, and the one that learning and development professionals can most directly influence to help ensure that e-learning is effective.

36. Design is important. It's about communicating effectively and facilitating more effective e-learning; it's not just about aesthetics.

37. There are two focuses in design: the learner, and the purpose of the learning. These, more than anything else, should determine the design strategy.

38. The five general principles of e-learning design are that it should be a managed programme; it should be an effective learning experience; it should be a learning process, not just e-reading; it should use technology to enhance learning; and it should exploit the strengths of the web.

39. The route map approach is the best way to design e-learning for models 1 and 2, and in some cases model 3. And there are useful design guidelines for all the models.

40. It is important to get the details right. It is important, too, to challenge design theory constantly. This is an evolving field where we do not yet have all the answers.

41. Evaluation is one of the four stages of the training cycle, following needs analysis, planning and preparation, and delivery; and one of the four essential elements of an e-learning strategy, along with strategy development, managing suppliers and resources, and design issues.

42. There are five main approaches to the evaluation of e-learning: Kirkpatrick's four levels, return on investment (ROI), return on expectations (ROE), Six Sigma, and total value-add.

43. Kirkpatrick's four levels – reactions, learning, behaviour and results – provide a long-standing contextual framework for understanding e-learning evaluation.

44. ROI describes the range of means of measuring the ratio of e-learning's costs to its benefits, and the return it yields to organizations, in financial terms.

45. ROE is about recognizing that value is defined by the customer and adjusting your evaluation strategy to meet this.

46. Six Sigma is a process for measuring the value of e-learning in terms that are meaningful to the business.

47. Total value-add describes the approach of recognizing all the different kinds of value e-learning can offer and ensuring that that contribution is recorded and recognized.

48. All these evaluation approaches may be applied to e-learning. Most of them are compatible, and your choice should be made on the basis of the best fit for your organization.

49. Learning and development professionals, and everyone interested in e-learning, need to learn more about e-learning and commit themselves to personal development with a view to implementing e-learning strategies and transforming e-learning for the future.

50. The final point. E-learning is here to stay, and will have an essential role in the future of learning. Nobody can afford to ignore it.

Glossary of technical terms in e-learning

The following is a brief summary of the meanings of the more common technical terms you are likely to encounter in e-learning. More information on each of them may be found through a web search, and especially by consulting sites that set out to explain the terms, such as http://en.wikipedia.org or http://www.webopedia.com or http://techdictionary.com.

ADL Advanced Distributed Learning, an initiative of the US Department of Defense, and the source of SCORM.

AICC Aviation Industry CBT Committee, a body that (among other things) sets standards for e-learning. More information at http://www.aicc.org.

ARIADNE Alliance of Remote Instructional Authoring and Distribution Networks for Europe, a body that (among other things) sets standards for e-learning. More information at http://www.ariadne-eu.org.

asynchronous e-learning Refers to learners learning at different times (cf **synchronous e-learning**).

authoring tool A software application that enables the non-techie to create e-learning content relatively easily.

avatar A virtual tutor, or animated character, who guides learners through a course of e-learning (and has wider applications on other websites).

bandwidth   The data rate, or communication speed, of an internet connection, with dial-up connections offering lower bandwidth and broadband offering more.

blog   Short for web-log, an online, usually multi-media, diary that allows feedback comments; a tool for interactive e-learning.

broadband   A high-speed internet connection that enables the user to access high-bandwidth content such as video.

bulletin board   See **discussion forum**.

CBT   Computer-based training, an old name for e-learning from before the advent of the internet, dating from when courses were stored on individual or networked computers or disks.

CD ROM   Stands for 'compact disk read-only memory'. A storage device of smaller capacity than a DVD, originally designed to store music, but can hold any kind of data; a typical CD ROM, often now abbreviated to just CD, can hold around 700 megabytes of data.

chat room   Or **chatroom**. A faster-paced version of a discussion forum. (As in a discussion forum, the 'chat' is typed and read, rather than spoken and heard.). Latterly eclipsed by developments in discussion forums and instant messaging, but sometimes loosely used as a collective term for all online discussion applications.

community of practice   A group of people with shared interests and experience cooperating over an extended period of time to learn together, often by means of e-learning.

courseware   Usually refers to the components of a course, such as text, images, animations, audio and video clips; can also be used as a collective term to refer to online courses and other learning opportunities.

discussion forum   Also known as a **bulletin board**. A place where multiple users can post comments by typing them into a set framework; a means for learners to contribute to discussions.

DVD   Digital versatile disk. A storage device for several gigabytes of content, large enough to store significant amounts of video content.

e-   A prefix standing for 'electronic', generally used to denote the computer- or internet-based version of any activity, such as e-learning.

e-assessment   The provision of tests (and other forms of assessment) online, including automated scoring.

e-portfolio   A means of collecting and maintaining evidence for assessment, online.

EPS   Electronic performance support, an e-learning model for providing on-the-job access to learner support.

Flash animation   The old brand term, still in common use, for the most popular form of animation software. Formerly owned by Macromedia, now owned by Adobe. One of the easiest ways of creating all sorts of moving images for e-learning.

formative assessment   Assessment 'as you go', designed to help the learner gauge his or her progress (cf **summative assessment**).

HTML   HyperText Mark-up Language, a code used by programmers to write web pages.

IEEE   Institute of Electrical and Electronics Engineers, a body that (among other things) sets standards for e-learning. More information at http://ltsc.ieee.org.

IMS   Or IMS Global Learning Consortium: Instructional Management System, a body that (among other things) sets standards for e-learning. More information at http://imsproject.org.

instant messaging   Online, 'real-time' communication tool, faster than e-mail, and for groups as well as one-to-one.

knowledge management   A concept closely related to e-learning, used to refer to the sharing and development, by people and organizations, of things they know. Some technologies support both knowledge management and e-learning.

learner management system (LMS)   A platform for managing information about learners, stored in a relational database, and generating management reports. Part of a **virtual learning environment**.

learning content management system (LCMS)   A platform for managing learning content, such as online courses, usually in the form of learning objects. Part of a **virtual learning environment**.

learning object   The smallest possible components of learning, such as single facts or formulae, that may be stored in a learning system and reused in order to make online courses with common elements easier to create.

learning platform   'Platform' is ICT jargon for a framework that allows software to run; in a learning context, this means the enabling technology for the e-learning – see **virtual learning environment**.

localization   The adaptation of e-learning produced in one nation or culture to other nations or cultures; may include language translation, currency conversion, style changes, different reference material, etc.

m-learning   Mobile learning, an unnecessary piece of jargon for e-learning accessed via mobile devices such as phones.

managed learning environment   Or managed learning system. An alternative name for a **virtual learning environment**.

metadata   Data about data. The 'tags' that help identify elements of e-learning to enable interoperability.

multi-media   A variety of media, such as audio, video, text and images, deployed in contexts such as e-learning.

open source   Refers to software that is not protected by copyright – the program's source code is open to all. In e-learning, software applications that may be acquired without paying a licence fee.

PDA   Personal digital assistant, a handheld device such as a BlackBerry, usually incorporating a mobile phone, with internet access, enabling mobile learning.

platform   A generic term for a software framework, including system architecture, operating systems and programming languages; in e-learning, a platform usually means a **virtual learning environment**.

podcast   An audio or video offer that may be accessed whenever the user chooses; distinct from a 'broadcast', and drawing on the word affinity with iPod, as it may be accessed via a handheld device.

PowerPoint   Microsoft's proprietary presentation software application, mainly used to create presentation slides.

rapid content development   The process whereby an author can relatively quickly and easily have e-learning ready for users.

reusable learning object   See **learning object**.

RSS   Really Simple Syndication, a process whereby users are alerted to the latest updates to a fast-changing website as they occur.

SCORM   Sharable Content Object Reference Model, a system for understanding how the many and varied e-learning standards relate to each other.

screencast   A movie of a web page, useful especially in learning to use computer applications.

screenshot   A still image of a web page; useful especially in learning to use computer applications.

Second Life   An internet-based virtual world (see **virtual reality**) where users can 'live', 'work', learn and undertake all kinds of virtual experiences.

simulation   Or Sim, for short. A way of artificially representing or modelling events or behaviours, offering a safe or secure way of learning while being as close as possible to the real thing. Flight simulators for aeroplane pilots are a well-known example, but e-learning has created a whole new generation of examples.

summative assessment   The assessment that 'sums up' a piece of learning by giving a final test of what the learner has learned. Usually deployed as a judgement of a learner's attainment, such as for a qualification.

synchronous e-learning   'Synchronized' learner participation; that is, learners learn at the same time (cf **asynchronous e-learning**).

T-learning   Television-based learning, an obscure and superfluous term for one possible application of e-learning.

USB flash drive   A data storage device that has much greater capacity than a CD ROM or DVD and is much more flexible to use. The name is somewhat of a misnomer, apart from the USB initials, which stand for 'universal serial bus' and refer to the connector.

virtual classroom   A means of holding live or 'synchronous' learning events online; part of a **virtual learning environment**.

virtual learning environment (VLE)   The most common name for an e-learning platform, which may include any or all of a **learner management system**, a **learning content management system**, an **authoring tool** and a **virtual classroom**.

virtual reality   A computer-simulated environment, either real or imaginary, which can have many applications (game playing is a common one), including learning.

webinar   A web-based seminar, or live e-learning event.

wiki   A website based on software that allows users to collaboratively create, edit, hyperlink, and organize the website's content.

WYSIWYG   What You See Is What You Get, a common acronym applied to applications such as authoring tools that do not require programming skills, because the author can see, as they write, exactly what the user will see.

XML   Extensible Mark-up Language, a code used by programmers to write web pages.

Index